STOP PLAYING SMALL

Turn obstacles into advantages and enjoy unapologetic success whilst building a creative business to be proud of!

JENNY DREW

authors
AND CO.

Disclaimer

I have tried to recreate events, locales and conversations from my memories of them. In order to maintain their anonymity in some instances I have changed the names of individuals and places, I may have changed some identifying characteristics and details such as physical properties, occupations and places of residence.

ISBN13: 979-8-829063-25-2 Paperback

ISBN13: 978-1-913728-76-2 Hardback

DEDICATION

This book is dedicated to my biggest cheerleaders - my mum and dad.

Thanks for always believing in and supporting my crazy ideas and dreams.

CONTENTS

INTRODUCTION

Stop playing small. Stop believing the opinions of society that say because you are a female in a creative business space, you are somehow less worthy of success - and I mean BIG success. Because it's all a lie. The only thing standing between you and MASSIVE GROWTH is yourself.

Being a creative can be tough. Owning a creative business can be even tougher. We have a ton of stereotypes to contend with. Apparently, we are scatty, heads in the clouds, total dreamers, poor, disorganised, perpetually underpaid... I could go on. However our good qualities FAR outweigh the bad. We are creators, master problem solvers, visionaries, bundles of energy and the best people to be around!

Add to the negatives the insult that what we do, regardless of how many years we have been honing our skills, or how many degrees we have, is massively undervalued by just about everyone, including your nearest and dearest - and probably yourself. The truth is, you have more creative talent in your baby toe than most people have in their entire body. You are highly skilled and what you can do is not common knowledge. It probably annoys you that people ask you to do things all the time but they do that because they believe they themselves are not capable of even beginning to learn or understand what you are capable of.

THEN, the cherry on top is we are also female, undervalued and underestimated by society from birth. So, is it any wonder that the business world is still dominated by men (and don't they know it!)? I believe you have been holding yourself back. The statistics about men applying for jobs when they fit 60% of the criteria, whereas women apply for jobs only when they hit 100% of the criteria, is evident at every stuffy networking event I have ever been to. I'm not saying you need to knock men down a peg or two; I'm saying you need to get better at walking in that room, taking a seat at the table, knowing you belong there and MAN, are they lucky to have you!

I want to empower you to want better for yourself... scrap that – to want THE BEST for yourself, and know that even against the odds, you are capable of absolutely amazing things and creating out-of-this-world experiences, and your creative business is the vehicle that's going to get you there.

Let's look at your business. It's making money, but you really are working for it. The dream of self employed life where you do exactly what you want, when you want, go on holiday whenever you like for stress free breaks was mis-sold to you -

by yourself, mainly. The work-life balance doesn't exist and you can't see a way off the hamster wheel you unknowingly built for yourself.

You feel like you own a job some days, not a business. You have a good business, maybe needs a few tweaks but the bones of it are good, so why isn't it growing as fast as you need it to? Why have you fallen into the trap of working all the hours of the day, too exhausted or stressed to enjoy your actual life? The only sure thing here is you've got a one way ticket to burn out and that is NOT why you started this business, nor something I would wish on anyone. Remember, you own the business, the business shouldn't own you.

I have been where you are. I have had days where I thought about packing it all in because it was too hard and wasn't worth it. I was supposed to be living the self employed, 'Instagram #girlboss' dream but instead, I was living in a stressy nightmare. I've been uncomfortable, I've made HUGE mistakes, I've experienced WILD sexism, I've had sleepless nights about money, I've been ripped off, I've played the victim, I've been a nightmare to be around and a crap friend, daughter and partner.

I've also turned every one of these things around into a positive. I've built an award-winning multi 6 figure business that employs 6 people, I own the UK's only sewing tuition franchise, I can work from anywhere and when I want. I've bought dream cars, handbags and manifested curly rescue dogs and husbands against all the odds (more on that later!). I'm typing this right now from a sun lounger in a private villa in Ibiza, worth 2M Euros. To be honest, I sometimes can't believe it myself. But one thing I know is it's my DUTY to help you get here too, much faster than me. I'm compressing a whole decade of creative business gems in here for you, to fast track your creation of the lifestyle you promised yourself in the beginning.

When you get on board with the teachings in this book, you'll see the glass ceiling you created for yourself disappear. Well, first you'll see it *appear* because you probably don't know it exists right now, and then we'll smash it up together whilst listening to Skunk Anansie or Alanis Morrisette, your choice!

You'll learn about the limitless possibilities and opportunities that are open to you and always have been (you just can't see them right now!). You won't be triggered by the underestimations that you will come across in your business life, instead you'll be spurred on by them!

You'll have a much needed community of like-minded business owners around you, you'll become more efficient with your time, giving you a healthier work-life balance and crucially, you'll be loving your life and your business again. These are my promises to you if you can implement the teachings in this book.

Speaking of teachings, what ARE you actually going to be learning?

You will learn about the importance of your own thoughts, being aware of them and taking charge of them. So many of us let our thoughts run wild and have never considered the damage they could be doing. Well that stops here.

I want to talk to you about being constantly underestimated and how you can turn it around to actually create positive change in your business.

You'll be getting out of the comfort zone and learning to seek out that uncomfortable feeling for the good of your own personal and business growth.

I'll be teaching you about the education trap you can fall into, how to find your business best pals, outsourcing to free your time and a whole load of mindset stuff around gratitude, money and pricing!

I'm also going to teach you how to become a pro at asking for and attracting help and assistance effortlessly because you better believe I didn't get here on my own!

Basically, if you were my best pal, this book is everything I would want you to know to ensure you start loving your life and your business again. All the stuff I wish I knew 10 years ago! Stick on the kettle or grab a wine; it's time to Stop Playing Small!

YOU'RE IN CHARGE OF YOUR OWN THOUGHTS

I know this might seem like a weird thing to say because, well, of course you are in charge of your own thoughts, right? They come from your brain, in your head and you are totally in control of them, end of chapter. Well, I'm here to tell you that you've been held hostage by your own brain, probably your whole life. You are about to become super aware of all the things that flit through your brain that do not serve you.

As a fellow creative, you undoubtedly have a wild imagination, you can see things in your mind's eye and you can visualise new projects, products, services and places easily. This is one of our strengths. We are born problem solvers, we enrich lives with our ideas, and ideas we have by the absolute shed load. This is all positive stuff but it also means we are excellent at imagining the million ways things can go wrong, or the horrible things people might be saying about us, or the swathes of people who are laughing at you for daring to succeed. This can REALLY hold you back and I know only too well about how your thoughts can spiral out of control and stop you from moving forward.

I used to be a catastrophiser. I don't even think that is a word but it's the only way to explain it. I would go to the worst case scenario with everything. And I mean EVERYTHING. It was an automatic thing, I had no control over it, or at least I didn't think I did.

I remember opening a second Sew Confident studio in a small, affluent area, just outside of Glasgow. It was before I franchised and I wanted to see if a second studio could work or if the Glasgow one was just some fluke (should really have had more faith in myself!). I found a space perfect for my classes and proceeded to negotiate the lease... having very little experience negotiating a lease (pay a solicitor to do it!). The landlord wanted a rent deposit AND a personal guarantee, which I know now is unusually heavy-handed for a low value rent, but I signed the 5-year lease anyway. Now, a personal guarantee meant I was personally liable for that rent, so if the company didn't work and went bust, I still needed to pay that rent. It was a Full Repairing and Insuring lease, which meant I was liable for any repairs to my part of the building too. Every single day I would think about the business failing and having to pay this rent myself. Or I would think about the entire roof caving in and having to pay to rebuild it. I was in the process of buying a house at the time and my thoughts spiralled to: what if they take my house? What if Steve leaves me because this implicates him too?

What if, when this studio closes, it affects my Glasgow studio and I lose everything? Do you want to know what the rent was on that studio? £300. THREE HUNDRED POUNDS a month. A figure btw, I could afford to pay personally. And the landlord had buildings insurance which would have covered any catastrophic roof issues. I had literally talked myself into a mess over an absolute worst-case scenario that was never going to happen. Guess what happened to the studio? It didn't work. It didn't work because every single day it was open, I was thinking about it failing and dreaming of being free from that personal guarantee I had signed. My thoughts had absolutely got the better of me and far from being harmless, they had actually caused me to fail. Looking back, could I make a success of that studio if I was to open it today? Absolutely... without the personal guarantee!

After this incident, you would think I would have had a lightbulb moment and noticed the link between thoughts and outcomes, but it took something far more extreme for me to finally wake up and start giving my thoughts and my mindset the attention they deserved.

There is a blurred line between business and personal life. I love what I do so much and my business is a massive part of my life, so some of the same unhelpful traits present in my business and my personal life. I was in Cyprus a few years ago, on holiday with Steve. One night, we were down in the hotel bar and a wee cat I had befriended jumped up and sat next to me. Then she jumped on my knee and sat purring away. I was delighted, having grafted to be this cat's pal all holiday. When she had had enough she jumped off my knee and scratched my leg by accident. Almost instantly I could feel the cloud of catastrophe appearing. In about one minute, my brain had pulled me out of this lovely evening on holiday and taken me to a place of "You're going to get toxoplasmosis". That night, I couldn't stop thinking about it. In bed, I struggled to get to sleep for thinking about it. In the middle of the night, I woke up shaking uncontrollably. I now know I was having a panic attack. I had got myself into such a mess over something that wasn't going to happen that I had actually caused a panic attack. After that holiday, I made a vow to sort out this unhelpful behaviour and get in control of my thoughts. If I could manifest those awful physical symptoms and blind panic from my thoughts then surely it works both ways and I can manifest amazing things through my thoughts too?

When I came home from that holiday, I was on a mission. I knew I needed help and guidance with this journey so I read all the books about mindset I could find, watched videos and worked with a mindset coach, Kirsty Ann Rae. The first step to being intentional with your thoughts is recognising that you are actually in control of them. You might not feel like it right now but you are and with practice, you can get better at it. Your negative thoughts are your brain's way of risk assessing situations. Taking the lease example: my brain knew that personal guarantee didn't sit well with me. I wasn't comfortable with it because the level of risk associated with it was not manageable for me at that time, even if it did seem a bit extreme. I didn't ask enough questions about the lease and I was intimidated by the official nature of it all. The mistake I made was not listening to my gut, and not negotiating better lease terms. I acknowledged the worst case scenario but didn't check in with myself to figure out if I was comfortable with it. If I was redoing that deal now, I wouldn't be signing that personal guarantee! Realising that your brain is like your risk averse best pal who ONLY has your best interests at heart is super helpful in not demonising your negative thoughts.

Everyone has these negative thoughts but not everyone dwells on them. You can't be super-happy-captain-positivity all the time, that's unrealistic and probably exhausting! But you can check in with yourself and be intentional about changing how you feel through your thoughts. There are two aspects that need to be addressed here. Internal and external factors. Let's look at internal factors first.

Right now, I want you to take a minute to acknowledge what's going on in your head. How are you feeling? Happy, calm, relaxed? Anxious, stressed, annoyed? If you are in the happy, calm, relaxed state, just take a second to really feel it. Be thankful for it. Store that feeling up and visualise yourself putting some of that positivity in a wee bottle for another day incase you need it. At this point it's also really nice to acknowledge what it is that's making you feel this way. Is the sun out? Did you just smash a big target? Did your best friend just send you an excellent cat meme? Whatever it is, acknowledge it and be grateful for the happy feelings

If you're leaning into the negative - anxious, stressed, annoyed - stop for a second. If you are at your desk, leave and sit somewhere nice and comfy, or go outside and get some fresh air. On a scale of 1-10 (1 being delighted and 10 being furious), note how you're feeling. Now try thinking about something that makes you happy or excited. Maybe you can visualise your dog gleefully playing in the garden or perhaps you can take yourself away to your favourite beach and take a minute to hear the sea and feel the sand on your feet. Spend a few minutes visualising something that makes you happy and really FEEL it. You know that excited feeling you get in your stomach before you go on a fab holiday? Or when you find out you were nominated for an amazing award? It will be different for everyone but find your thing. For me, holidays are always an easy way to lift my mood. I imagine floating about in a pineapple in the pool, Pina colada in hand, watching wee, wispy clouds float by. Or I take myself to the beach (mentally) and listen to the waves crashing. That's what you want to feel. Do it for about 5 minutes if you can. Now note how you feel on a scale of 1-10. I bet it's better than when you started!

Some people call this raising your vibration, all I know is THIS WORKS. Here's the thing - your brain doesn't actually know the difference between what's real and what's imagined.

In the mid 90's there was a study conducted where 3 groups of people took part in an experiment involving learning a simple piano sequence. One group physically practised, one group just visualised practicing and the other group did nothing (were they the control, or just lazy? I don't know). During the experiment they scanned each groups brains, specifically looking at the areas related to the finger muscles.

There was no change in the control group, as expected. There was a change in the group who physically practised the piano, as expected as they were actually moving their fingers and learning the sequence. Amazingly, the group who visualised the sequence had the same changes in their brain as the group who physically did the exercise. How unbelievably cool is that?

When I first found out about this, I was amazed, then terrified. Firstly, I was amazed that I was actually so in control of my brain and with this kind of knowledge, could use this amazing part of my anatomy to my advantage. This was closely followed by a brief period of absolute fear because of course, with my catastrophising ways not yet under control, I was immediately aware of how much damage I could potentially do by thinking about exclusively negative things all the time. I am actually rolling my eyes at the old me, I was such a buzz kill! But the truth is, knowledge is power and once you know how incredibly powerful you are when you're in control of your own thoughts, the sky really is the limit. How many well known sayings or clichés can I fit into one sentence, eh? Two, apparently.

I have another story about a time when my negative thoughts managed to completely override my positive ones and cause something physical to happen. When I was building my business I had many jobs on the side in the early days. One was in a fab gift shop in town, Maia Gifts. I bought this ceramic bank shaped like a Boston terrier one day, wrapped it in bubble wrap and as I was leaving, my work pal made a joke about "watch you don't smash it to bits on the way home!". Well, all I could think about all the way was smashing this lovely little bank to smithereens. Every time I walked past a lamppost, I imagined cracking the bank against it, every time I walked past someone, I imagined them falling into me, me losing my balance, falling over and smashing it. It was RIDICULOUS, that's literally never happened to me before. I got to just outside my flat at the time, amazed nothing had happened to the wee bank. I still had the concrete stairs to negotiate though, three flights of them. I made it up all the stairs, tripped on the very top one, fell over and smashed the bank outside my front door. Now, I can have a big LOL at this now but there is no doubt in my mind that I absolutely manifested that. I thought about it so intensely, I imagined tripping up the stairs as I went. I could hear my pal warning me not to smash it. It had been written in the stars as soon as I left work... by me.

You might be thinking, well someone else started that ball rolling by saying it was going to smash before I left. But like the chapter says, YOU are in charge of YOUR own thoughts. You and you only decide what to dwell on, what to take on board, what to bin and ultimately, how you feel. I could have said "oh thanks very much, you jinxed me, it's your fault" but owning your own thoughts and resulting actions or feelings starts with full responsibility for your own self.

What could I have done in that situation to stop the thoughts spiralling? There is an Neuro Linguistic Programming(NLP) tip that my good friend and fellow business owner, Margaret Shenken, told me about. It's designed to stop you spiralling out of control with your thoughts and it is so simple! All you have to do when you feel yourself going down a negative road in your mind is to visualise a big red stop sign and if you can, say the word "STOP" out loud. This is a little bit of a wake up call and will bring you back into the present. It's called a pattern interrupt and stops your brains automatic pilot by pulling you out of a learned spiral. The same way you can drive to work and have no recollection of actually getting there - your brain is running programmes and habits in the background all the time; some are less helpful than others and need to be interrupted to stop the spiral into a pit of misery. Maybe a pit of misery is a bit extreme but I really want you to take this on board and start getting really intentional about becoming aware of and breaking these negative spirals!

All I have told you so far is my experience of things going wrong as a result of my thoughts but what about some examples of when I have put these learnings into practice and things have gone right? Back in 2016/17 I had joined a business accelerator programme and it was the first time I really felt like I had found my people. They were super positive, driven, absolute go-getters and I just loved being around them. A lot of them were applying for a business competition called Scottish Edge. It's an amazing business competition with BIG financial prizes for business that can demonstrate new and exciting products, services or business models (highly recommend looking into it if you are a Scottish-based business!). They have various categories and one is for the under 30s which at the time I was. The prize then was £10k and funnily enough, that was pretty much exactly what I needed to build the franchise model, which is why I was in that business accelerator in the first place. So I decided to go for it. The application was pretty gruelling but, these things are difficult in order to separate the wheat from the chaff. If you can't be bothered even putting the time into the application, you don't deserve the place on the competition. When something is difficult, I actually see it as a positive because most people will give up half way through, which means less competition for me - how's that for turning something on its head, eh! So I stuck at it. Once I submitted my giant application, including a video recording of my 3 minute pitch, I found out I got through to the next round, which was pitching live in front of a panel of judges. Terrifying - especially when so much rested on this. From that moment I started visualising the end result I wanted which was me, on stage, collecting that trophy and seeing that £10k in my bank. I visualised every day. I FELT the emotions of winning, I saw the money in my bank account and it was already spent in my head. I practised my pitch and got fellow business pals to fire questions at me to prepare me for the final hurdle. I know 3 minutes doesn't sound like much but when you are trying to memorise a pitch, it's actually quite difficult. I mean, I can still remember all the words to an entire All Saints album from 1996 (including Shaznay's raps), but remember a 3 minute speech on a business I know inside out? Forget about it! In hindsight, I probably should have just rapped it. I actually messed up the pitch a bit, I forgot a bit and it totally threw me off but I figured a little bit of them feeling sorry for me standing up there like a deer in the headlights might actually help matters. I didn't let it put me off. The physical work from my part was done but the visualisation work was still ongoing. Every day I was letting myself get excited about winning, feeling that excited feeling in my stomach and forging ahead with the franchising plans. I remember I was driving when all the results came through via email. My friend phoned me and asked if my results were through and I immediately pulled over (when it was safe to do so obviously, in case any traffic cops are reading this). I had won! And it felt exactly how I had imagined! A wonderful combination of putting the work in and visualising the success had pushed me right over that winning line and it felt so good!

What about those external factors I spoke about earlier? I've already mentioned that you are in control of your own thoughts and, if you haven't already, it's time to start taking responsibility for everything that happens in your life, good and bad. This can be a really hard pill to swallow for some people, either because you've had a tough life or because you enjoy being in that victim state. The former I can sympathise with, although I still don't agree with it, but the latter I have zero time for. I will either call out your victim mentally or distance myself from you. I can't deal with it. If you regularly feel hard done by or that things aren't fair and you use it as an excuse for why you are not doing what you should be doing or getting to where you want to be, then you have a victim mentality and I want you to pledge to pull yourself out of that state today, for the sake of your own progress and happiness. Awful things happen to people all the time. Great things happen to people all the time. Mediocre things happen to people all the time and that is called life. What I'm talking about here is are you going to let life happen to you or are you going to wade through all the nonsense and blaze your own trail *despite* what has happened to you?

I used to be very reactive emotionally. I didn't think, I just acted on primal instinct. This made me a bit of a fiery character. I had some pretty upsetting things happen in my family life back in about 2012, the likes of which had never happened before in my little harmonious family unit and it knocked me for six. I was furious all the time and it was eating me up! I don't believe it was a coincidence that led me to work with my now friend Soni, in the gift shop, Maia Gifts, I was talking about earlier. Soni and his partner Sam are the picture of serenity. They are spiritual and the kind of people who have this infectious calm energy. Officially, I was an employee but looking back, I probably felt like more of a client. I was getting little gems of therapy every day in that shop (which, btw, you should visit in Glasgow or online. It's adorable) and I didn't realise at the time that what they were introducing me to was going to stay with me for the rest of my life. One day, Soni told me a story about reincarnation and how every life was another chance for you to do the right thing and learn from your past mistakes. Bearing in mind I was in full victim mode and didn't think I had actually done anything wrong, I did start to come round to this idea. He said you essentially have a filing cabinet from your past life. And even though you might come back as someone else, you have these same files in your cabinet that either stay with you until the next life (which means living through it again) or you learn to behave differently and the file is removed. The end goal being to reach Nirvana, where Kurt Cobain sings you to sleep every night. Ok that bit isn't true but it started getting a bit heavy so I had to add in a joke. For my specific issue, Soni and Sam showed me that the only person who was being damaged by my anger and resentment was me. It was physically showing up in the form of frequent palpitations, and not being able to sleep, and a really annoying twitchy eyelid! To "remove this file", I had to apologise to the people I was angry with for whatever I had done to them in this life or a past life. I only had to apologise in my head, but I had to really mean it. Part of this exercise for me was seeing this situation from the other side and understanding the other people's legitimate reason for behaving how they did. Although these folk are no longer in my life, I genuinely wish them the best and actually I now know that this awful situation had to happen in order for me to learn this valuable lesson, which changed me for the better indefinitely. I'm still not always amazing at this - it can take months or even years for me to reach this conclusion - but I do always try to get there eventually.

I believe this way of thinking really serves you in a business capacity too. If you can get on board with pushing your emotions out of the way and seeing things from the other party's perspective, it enables you to make decisions based on facts rather than emotion. Whether you are having a disagreement with a supplier, employee or a customer, being able to remove yourself from that will help you make the right decision for you and the business! I quite often find myself asking "What is the lesson in this?" when things aren't going to plan. I recently had a bit of "beef" with a business local to my studio and the lesson there was that I had completely outgrown that space and wasn't aligned to the environment or the people anymore, so rather than get mad I saw it as a sign that leaving (I was in the process of doing this anyway) was absolutely the right decision!

Awareness of your own behaviour and why you act the way you do is key here. It can be eye opening and you might need some help along the way in the form of some friends intervening or some therapy sessions with someone. I actually believe everyone should invest in therapy, both for personal and business reasons. It will certainly help you take charge of your own thoughts!

BEING UNDERESTIMATED AND WHAT TO DO ABOUT IT

As a women in business, or even a women on the planet, I believe we are grossly underestimated by our peers, by our family and worst of all, by ourselves! During my 10 years in business, I have been on a journey of massive self-discovery and I'm still on that journey. One of the most useful things I have learned - and used to my advantage - is being consistently underestimated by just about everyone I know and meet. The good news here is when you're underestimated the only way is up, the bad news is you're gonna have to fight to be taken seriously in a lot of rooms that matter to you and learn to let it go in the rooms that don't... and I'm only now getting the hang of this.

I could probably write a whole book on the experiences in business and in my personal life where I have felt undervalued. It has always evoked the same fighting response in me. I don't know if I was born with a fighting spirit or if I learned it was the best way to go but my earliest memory of my "I will show you" mentality comes from secondary school. I was an all-rounder in school to be honest. Arty obviously, good at English (you can be the judge of that based on how many grammatical errors you can find in this book!), good at biology but not so good at maths. Now, I use maths every single day of my life. I use it when working out margins, when calculating the pattern for a circle skirt, when drawing to scale plans for a new premises - I literally use it every day. But maths in school lost me when the teacher couldn't explain why we were doing something. I remember being told "that's just how it's done", which to my logical brain was not an explanation I could get on board with. Thankfully, I sat next to my mathematical whizz kid best pal, Amy, in standard grade Maths, so I managed to scrape a 2 (I will never know how but I'll take it, thanks - it's the second best grade). When I announced to my teacher that I wouldn't be taking higher maths, he retorted "You'll never get anywhere in life without Maths". Cue my first experience of a man standing in front of me telling me I couldn't do something and forcing me to make a silent promise in my mind that I was going to make it my life's mission to be wildly successful. Look at me now Mr. Miller, doin' alright for a Higher-Maths-Heathen, eh? Maybe I should thank him because he ignited something I've never been able to put out.

I have learned that every negative experience has a positive lesson or takeaway. Having this state of mind enables you to sail through all the crap that is inevitably going to be chucked at you on your business journey. If a deal doesn't go to plan, what direction are you being pushed in instead? I believe the universe carves a path for you based on what you want, think about and visualise. However, I also know it's not as easy as being like "cool, this awful thing has happened but I am impossibly positive and immediately understand why it's happening". It might take a few days or weeks or even years for you to understand that everything that is happening to you is happening for a reason.

I've not always been ZENny Drew, let me tell you! And to be honest, some would tell you I'm still not, but I don't allow myself to act on knee jerk reactions anymore which is definitely a sign of my business, and probably personal, maturity.

The maths example isn't really anything to do with being female and is definitely nothing to do with business. There isn't a female business owner I know, however, who hasn't experienced some kind of judgement based on being just that. The situation is definitely improving and I see it as our duty to speak about our experiences so other emerging female entrepreneurs can acknowledge it's happening to them and absolutely smash it in business regardless.

One of my biggest areas of annoyance is in commercial property. Between chauvinistic pig landlords and old school property agents, the whole industry needs to be turned on its head. Yes, I've had decent landlords but the bad grossly outweighs the good. Let me tell you some stories.

When I was two years into business and looking for my first studio, I had messaged a few people to view some places. To say I was green was an understatement, I didn't really know what to expect to be honest. I told the landlord what my business was, the kind of space I needed to teach in and he showed me a glorified cupboard space. I mean, I couldn't have fit two staff in there, never mind classes of eight. He said he had another space but it was "very expensive" and he was reluctant to show me it. How about you just show your spaces, tell me your prices and then let me decide what's best?! In his defence, he was a great landlord in every other respect but his initial assumptions about what I, as a female business owner, could afford were definitely noted. I took the bigger space of course and it really wasn't that expensive.

A few years later, I was looking for a new premises just outside Glasgow. Still pretty green when it comes to property, I had found the perfect place... which actually turned out not to be the perfect place. This was the deal I spoke about in the last chapter where I signed the personal guarantee and I couldn't sleep at night as a result. The first sign this was a terrible idea was when the solicitor I had decided to use accidentally copied me in on an email saying she had "made a rod for her own back" by saying she would look over my lease for £300. Bitching about me to the landlord's solicitor... YAY for the sisterhood! She also neglected to tell me that signing a personal guarantee and having a deposit was incredibly heavy-handed and unnecessary but it's a lesson I will never forget.

Meanwhile, I was getting snippy voicemails from the landlord telling me to hurry up and he was going to give the premises to someone else. Let me tell you what I know now, commercial leases take MONTHS to negotiate. Do not let anyone push you into signing anything you're not happy with or haven't sought legal advice on. Always be prepared to walk away! However, I didn't have anyone telling me this then and I was all caught up with not wanting to inconvenience the landlord, not wanting to make him think I was messing him around (when I wasn't!), and trying to seem as professional as possible. The snippy voicemails continued and I genuinely did not know how to deal with it. I was probably about 27 at the time and still honestly intimidated by men in property and he clearly knew this. I felt so uncomfortable dealing with this man that I had to ask my dad to help me with the whole situation. Looking back, I am FURIOUS at myself - I should have told him where to stick it - but back then I thought it was just how it was.

About a year later, I wanted out and found someone to take over the lease. There was a clause that allowed me to essentially sell the lease to someone else with the landlords permission. The contract also stated that my £1500 deposit would be returned after I left, assuming I hadn't wrecked the place, which of course, I hadn't. We had a meeting before I left where the landlord told me he would not be returning my deposit AND I had to pay £450+vat for a new lease for the new tenant. I was so intimidated by his cocksureness that the only thing I could say was I would need to think about it. To cut a long story short, after emails back and forward, with him making up other charges, I enlisted the help of a massive law firm (my turn to be intimidating), they sent him a demand letter stating that everything he was saying and attempting to charge was completely illegal and he had to return the money. I then got an email from him feigning surprise that I had gone down the legal route with him, saying he thought we were on friendly terms. Nope, bye! Days later, a cheque arrived for all the money he owed me.

Unfortunately for him, he underestimated me. He didn't think I would fight it and I hope he never treats another woman like that again. I forgive him. I'm sure he had his reasons, and it must have been annoying for him to have to vet a new tenant so soon. Perhaps he thought he was playing by the rules and had been ill advised - I will never know! Remember contracts are there to protect both parties – yes, they are often landlord sided but they offer protection for you too.

What's the lesson for us here? Firstly, you don't know what you don't know! That's why property solicitors exist - just make sure you get a good one. Secondly, you don't have to bow down to someone because they have more money than you, have been in business longer than you or talk a better game than you. If you're not comfortable with the way someone speaks to you either get someone else to come with you to the meeting as support or tell them calmly you're not comfortable being spoken to like that. If one of my franchisees came to me now with this story, where a landlord was sending snippy voicemails, I would tell them to walk away.

How someone else treats you is a reflection of them, not a reflection of you, don't forget that!

More recently, I have found myself back in the property zone. It's like a bloody pit of piranhas! This time though, I knew I actually had to do some work on my own self-confidence in this space. I spoke to my coach, Kirsty Anne Rae, who has always helped me with limiting beliefs. I reckon "I will always end up getting humped on property deals" is a pretty big limited belief in a bricks and mortar business so I needed to do something about it. She did her NLP, Hypnotherapy magic and soon after, it was put to the test.

I won't go into the details because it was actually very boring but I had yet another man in property giving me snippy chat on the phone. He had messed up some numbers and as a result was expecting me to agree to paying more rent because "I was still getting a really good deal". At the time of the call, I was sitting next to my now husband, who works with these kind of people day in, day out. At one point he was biting his own knuckle incredulously trying not to butt in. I stayed cool, didn't get emotional, didn't feel intimidated and told him I would get back to him once I had thought about it. Steve was ragin'. He couldn't believe anyone would speak to anyone in a professional setting the way he spoke to me. And I honestly felt vindicated that what I have been feeling and experiencing in this sector is NOT the norm for men and is unacceptable. And it made me realise this chapter right here is one of the most important in the book. Because if it's happening to me in all parts of my business, then I know it's happening to you too. And if we keep putting up with it and accepting it as the norm then it won't change for us or the women a few steps behind us.

So, how DO we deal with being underestimated all the time? I now see it as an opportunity. I used to go to networking events and have people tell me my sewing tuition business was "cute" and "lovely" and "it must be nice to sew all day" and "can you take my trousers up". I have no doubt this, along with all the other comments, MADE me start the UKs only sewing tuition franchise. It MADE me grow my team. It MADE me increase my turnover, year on year, to multi 6 figures and it MADE me stop playing small. You can make silent pacts with yourself that the next time you see that person, they're going to be dying to know how you did it, so they can do it too. And there is something so satisfying about shocking someone with your success.

I have had countless conversations with people in all walks of business and all I'm thinking in my head is "you're speaking to me like I'm a daft wee girl". I don't doubt you have experienced this too. I now remove myself from these conversations. You don't need to politely nod your head, stuck in a boring conversation with someone who doesn't interest you. Your time is precious, don't waste it stuck in conversations with people who monopolise your time. I hereby give you absolute permission to leave those conversations, the excuse of needing another cup of tea is my go to get out and I do, in fairness, usually need another cup of tea so it's also not a lie!

There is also something to be said for picking your battles here too. There are some people I meet and I think "I don't really care what you think" and I'll let it go, and there are other people I'll meet and I know I'll meet them again down the line, and those are the ones I choose to spur me on. I should also put here that I am pretty much exclusively talking about business contacts. Family and friends are a whole other ball game.

Your nearest and dearest can be your biggest cheerleaders or your greatest critics and it usually comes from a place of love even if it's the latter. If you are reading this book, you are on a journey of self-development. A journey that most people will never go on. You're intentionally trying to better yourself, change your mindset, open your world up to the wildest opportunities. This is scary for a lot of people. You're not towing the line here, you're venturing into the unknown and you're going places your friends and family might not be going and that's scary for them sometimes. Out of love they might try to reign you in. Your job is to reassure them and keep going anyway. Because as soon as you start to see success and they start to see that you're capable of dealing with the obstacles that you'll inevitably find on this incredible journey, they will become your biggest cheerleaders. You might find you become a trailblazer of hope for a better, more abundant life.

I get a real kick out of seeing that little glimmer of hope appear on the face of someone who has realised that if you can do it, they can too. For so long, my friends have almost certainly thought I was a bit mad. I think we are all a bit mad in the business world, don't you? I believe that if you can inspire even just one person to believe there is a more abundant life waiting for them, then you should grab that opportunity with both hands. I know that some of my beliefs are so far-fetched for my friends and family that they will never get on board with them. Some of their beliefs are too different from mine for me to understand too - this works both ways.

I remember opening my mind to Feng Shui and Crystals after joining a session with the wonderful Sarah Stone (who is such a ray of light - I was so inspired by her Feng Shui journey!). Shortly afterwards I bought some crystals, a wee money tree and I rearranged my desk for optimal Feng Shui. I had no idea if it was going to work but I am an eternal optimist and figure if it can work for someone else, it could work for me too. My focus was definitely on this little money tree. I had mentioned it to my best friends and they had had a wee laugh about me actually planting something in the garden and waiting for the £50 notes to grow. I am not exactly known for my green fingers. It was, of course, a little crystal tree with an agate base, copper trunk and amethyst and citrine 'leaves' (I'll add a link to the one I have to jennydrew.com!). I was just about to go into launch mode of a brand new online course. I looked at this little tree every day. I dusted it, I touched its little leaves and I imagined it drawing in good fortune for my launch. I did a whole load of other things too, like getting laser focussed on my launch goals, really listening to what my customers needed and tracking my and the teams progress every day. That launch brought in £56k. The most money I had ever made in one week. The most money I had ever made from an online class launch and it HAD to have something to do with the money tree and the crystals and the new Feng Shui desk set up.

Over the next few weeks, there was a sudden interest from my friends in the mysterious money tree. In the possibility that there was more to good fortune than luck and grafting. That there was something in handing over a little bit of the control over your life and your finances to an unknown power you don't fully understand, whilst simultaneously doing the work. The day after my friend Linzi received her money tree, she had a mysterious note through her front door. It was lined paper wrapped around a £10 note! She couldn't believe it! When she opened the note however she discovered it was actually a hand written note from the local Jehovah's Witnesses and a pamphlet that happened to be the exact same colour as a Scottish tenner (GENIUS MARKETING JW, 1-0!). I wish I could print colour pictures in this book to show you, it was hilarious, but if you go to Jennydrew.com/bookbonus, I will add the photo there for you to see. Obviously the money tree doesn't make people post tenners through your door but the fact that Linzi's brain went straight to that actually demonstrates how something like this does work. And I love her for getting so on board with it! It opens your mind to opportunities and ideas related to money. It puts your brain on high alert where before these opportunities wouldn't have even registered with you. Anyway, I have gone off on a money tree tangent there because I love them so much - I knew this would happen!

Being underestimated by people who love you and people who don't know you is an opportunity. An opportunity for your own growth and an opportunity for you to inspire other people to try something new. Yes, it can be pretty infuriating at times and it's ok to feel that way but as long as you end up seeing it for what it is, pushing for change in behaviours and mindsets and being a trailblazer for what is possible, then you will be able to say, hand-on-heart, that being underestimated pushed you to be a better version of yourself. To stop playing small.

GETTING OUT OF THE COMFORT ZONE

I'm not sure who it was that first introduced me to the now very commonly used term "out of the comfort zone is where the magic happens" but it's probably the most useful piece of wisdom I have ever been given.

I want to be really clear here that I don't mean taking massive unmitigated risks and waiting for that magic to appear. You can be a sensible, risk averse person and still push the boundaries and make massive progress. In fact, I would go as far to say if you are a risk averse person, as I am, then this advice is going to change the course of your business and your life.

If I think back to the first time I choose to leave my comfort zone, I reckon it was in my adult life. I wasn't a risk taker as a child, I was pretty shy most of the time. I followed most of the rules (ha!), did as I was told, finished school, went to uni, ticked all the boxes. When I left uni with no real career progression in sight, I was angry that I had towed the line, taken all the advice, played it a bit safe and still ended up in a bit of a hopeless career position. I definitely ended up with a bit of a victim mentality at this point and proof that playing it safe makes for a dull life! If you can recognise yourself in this victim state, you need to start working your way out of it ASAP. I have a whole guide for digging yourself out of the victim hole on the website www.jennydrew.com/bookbonus.

How do you recognise when you're in the victim state? You probably say things like "that's just my luck", "bad things happen to me all the time" and "it's not my fault". If this resonated with you, you need to take action right now. I'm going to tell you some things that you don't want to hear. I'm going to say some things that I can guarantee the people around you want to say but are too scared to.

Take responsibility for your own life, and everything in it - good and bad. Right now.

If you're in this state, this is uncomfortable for you. THIS is you leaving your comfort zone. The only person in the driving seat of your life is you. The victim mentality feels good because nothing is your problem, it's all out of your hands, life happens to you and there's nothing you can do about it but moan when it's unpleasant. You get attention from other people by being in this state. People feel sorry for you, they offer to help you, they make excuses for you so you don't have to. You never have to wake up and think "bloody hell, I need to take action to change this". It's weird that your brain would reward you for these damaging behaviours but it does and the feeling is addictive. Recognise this.

You're going to have to trust me when I say that the grass is most certainly greener on the other side. Usually it isn't, but this time it most certainly is. But it's uncomfortable getting there. Be honest with yourself and list all the positives you get from your current state. You never have to share this with anyone and you can rip it up straight away but acknowledge that there are some rewards. Then list the flip side negatives.

For example:

> Positive: It feels good in the moment
> Negative: Long term it feel hopeless
>
> Positive: You get attention from people
> Negative: People eventually grow tired of it
>
> Positive: It's someone else's problem
> Negative: You are not in control of your own life

From my own experience, the first step of changing any mindset is actually acknowledging that it is a choice you are making every day and deciding enough is enough.

The second step is being aware of your inner monologue and how you speak to and about yourself out loud:

Change "That's just my luck" to "This happened but these two great things also happened!" Change "Nothing ever goes right for me" to "That wasn't meant for me but I know it's pushing me in another direction full of opportunity!"

Change "It's not my fault" to "I wonder how I can change the outcome of that next time?"

This might seem like a ridiculous exercise but the way you speak to and about yourself is so important in influencing your mood and your mindset. In business, you really need to get used to things not going your way because it happens all the time. Sometimes it's small things that you can move on from quickly but sometimes it's massive, overarching nightmares that need to be addressed head on. The overarching nightmares often put me into a temporary victim state. Now it probably takes me a few days to process the problem, process how I am feeling about it, process why I am feeling that way and then ultimately acknowledge that the only person who can steer the business back into the right path is me. Sometimes there is a self-pity duvet day (or three) thrown in there for good measure because I do believe you need to feel everything and get all your emotions out. Thereafter, I find it really helpful to have the faith that whatever direction I was going in wasn't for me, to try to see the direction I am being pushed in instead and throw myself into it.

I've got some other hints and tips about how to take control of your life again on the website;

www.jennydrew.com/bookbonus

I use these tactics on a monthly basis as staying positive all the time is impossible and your mindset and your mental health is a constant work in progress that needs to be nurtured.

I really, SERIOUSLY, digressed there into almost a whole chapter about victim mentality. I only know so much about it because in those darkish days after uni, I was the embodiment of the victim. I can spot it in other people a mile off too and I still sometimes dip into it myself. The first time I can really remember properly feeling like I wanted to run away screaming from a situation I had put myself forward for was back in 2016, when I applied for a business accelerator programme. I had just realised that I couldn't do what I wanted to do without help. And as if by magic (some might say law of attraction, eh!) an advert for this business accelerator appeared on my Facebook. I had decided I wanted to franchise; the business was doing well but I needed help growing. I applied and got an interview and to my horror, the interview requirement was a 60 second pitch. A what now? I had never done one of these and it brought back the fear of doing talks to the class at school and uni - I didn't enjoy public speaking at all. I could have just ignored it and continued what I was doing but something in me, although I felt sick at the thought, knew that if I wanted to get anywhere I had to do things that other people might not do. I did the interview, it didn't go half as bad as I thought it would and I got in! Everything about this accelerator was uncomfortable. The networking was new to me and pretty uncomfortable. The constant pitching in front of everyone was excruciating (but it is a really good way to tell people about your business quickly!). The meetings where your business gets deconstructed and critiqued were initially really difficult to listen to. But this one step changed the entire direction of the business, it changed me as a person and as an entrepreneur, and it introduced me to some of the most amazing, driven, sometimes absolutely bananas business owners, a lot of whom I am still great friends with today. This was levelling up, this was getting out of the comfort zone and it was just the start.

In the following months, I discovered I was actually pretty good at pitching. I used to have to do it all the time. I would get taken to events with a few other prized pitchers and wheeled out as an example of how it was done. I was learning how to stand, how to breathe to convey confidence. I was even doing wonder women poses in secret before I was going on (google it, it works!). As I grew in confidence and continued to work towards my goal of franchising the business, there were a lot of fellow entrepreneurs who were applying for a competition called Scottish Edge. This is a business pitching competition where you can win money if you can prove your idea has legs, is innovative and that you will go on to create jobs and opportunities for others in the future. I was under 30 so there was a special Young Edge category I could apply for that involved a massive application form, a video pitch and then, if successful, a live 3-minute pitch in front of a panel of judges. Absolutely bloody terrifying! But the prize was £10k and mentoring and help from Scottish Edge afterwards. It was exactly what I needed! I spent months on the application. I definitely had fleeting thoughts about packing it in because it was so difficult, but I got loads of guidance from friends from the accelerator who had applied before. I also kept telling myself that THIS is what separates the wheat from the chaff. They don't want half-arsed applications from half-arsed applicants. I had to be prepared to do what other business owners weren't to get ahead and open up new opportunities. This is out of the comfort zone again.

I remember on pitch day being the world's most nervous person. I had put so much work into this; I NEEDED this to move the business to the next level. I'd love to say my 3-minute pitch went without a hitch but it didn't. I messed it up right in the middle, like a deer in the headlights. The interesting thing you realise when this happens is how much the panel were vying for you. Contrary to being the Dragon's Den panel of unimpressed faces, all I could see was encouragement on their faces. I got back on track, answered some of their difficult questions and left knowing I had done my best. Fast forward a few weeks, I found out I had won the £10k and it all stemmed from taking that first leap into the unknown of joining that accelerator. THIS was the magic people talked about. It was real and it was happening to me!

Fast forward to more recent times. At the end of 2020, mid-pandemic, I decided that rather than staying in survival mode (I had been wallowing there since March 2020, along with a lot of other exhausted business owners), I was going to join a mastermind. I needed to get in the room with people who were smashing it, more than I was. I wanted to meet people who were steps ahead of me so I could benefit from their energy, be inspired by their actions and grow my already amazing group of business friends. I already knew about Lisa

Johnson and I had done one of her courses, put into action her teachings and made a chunk of money off the back of it. I knew what she was teaching was legit because I had done it myself so it seemed like a safe bet for me to apply to join her mastermind. It wasn't cheap - a 5-figure sum - but I am a firm believer that you get what you pay for and I believed I would easily make back my investment (which I did, 2 months later!). When I joined, I was plagued with imposter syndrome. Did I belong here? Were these my people? Did anyone like me? I know self-doubt is a sign I'm pushing the boundaries of what's comfortable and I knew it was something I had to work through. Also, most of these things don't matter. Did I belong here? Yes I did, as much as anyone else who has paid to be there. Were these my people? There were about 40 of them, statistically one of them would be! Did anyone like me? This was my inner 5-year-old having a wee wobble, of course someone would like me, I'M GREAT... and you know, statistically speaking... haha! I recognised it for what it was. It was another levelling up.

The mastermind included some trips away with everyone. Because we were mid pandemic, the first trip to Croatia was looking less and less likely the closer it got. In the end, I was considering FedExing myself to Croatia if it meant getting out of the country, but I think even FedEx stopped flying there so it wasn't to be. There was so much back and forward, with flights getting cancelled left right and centre, that quite a few people decided that the whole thing was such a nightmare - between flights and all the changing Covid rules - that they opted out of the whole thing. A small group of people I had never met before were still up for doing something though. Never one to pass up the opportunity to go abroad, I was tentatively up for this. There was talk of hiring a villa in Ibiza and all meeting out there to write our books together - this very book! Some of the group had contacts in the property world and could get us booked in a fab villa. Was I really considering going abroad alone, during a pandemic, to meet absolute strangers, in a private villa, in the middle of nowhere (or Santa Eularia, whatever)? Well yes, I was.

I was having doubts about this trip up until the moment I stepped on the plane. Hell, up until the moment I got out of the taxi at the villa. So many things could have gone wrong. The catastrophising part of my brain was going into overdrive! They all could have been horrors for a start. What if I didn't like them? What if they didn't like me? But then, what if they were amazing and I made lifelong pals? My contingency plan that I always have, was, if it all went tits up, I would leave and go have a lovely week in a hotel in Ibiza on my own and when the worst case scenario involves reading books on a sun lounger, sipping a cocktail in Ibiza, you can pretty much always count me in. Here's what happened - I was greeted at the door by Sarah, with a gin in hand for me and I knew then these were my people. We had the best week! We went to Lio, this wonderfully bougie cabaret place (definitely go next time you're in Ibiza), we cycled round Formentera, we fixed each others business quandaries, we had Debbie's 40th Birthday celebrations there, we ate in some of the best restaurants and we lazed around in the sun in our luxury 2 million euro villa. I remember my mum saying when I came home that she thought I wasn't enjoying myself because I wasn't really posting anything on social media, but the opposite was true. I was out there living my best, social media free (mostly) life and soaking up every minute of it!

It's not always monetary value that comes from getting out of the comfort zone. Prior to this, I think I attributed pushing the boundaries with financial gain because it's what my experience was. On this trip, I learned that I was capable of doing something that most people wouldn't dream of doing (in a pandemic). I made genuine life-long friendships with these people through an amazing shared experience that none of us will ever forget. I lazed around in the most expensive villa I have ever stepped foot in, let alone stayed in. I got a little taste of what was possible for my life and it was as if the universe was giving me a sneaky peak of what the future holds should I continue to put my faith in it.

At this point I would also like to confirm that pretty much ZERO of my book was actually written in Ibiza apart from the chapter titles and the intro... and I believe that was the same for Sarah, Debbie and David. And we all had the same worries about turning up and living with three potential madskulls for a week - so at least I wasn't alone with that thinking either!

The one takeaway I want for you from this chapter is to be mindful of your mindset and the effect it can have on your life, both positive and negative. Don't float along, letting life happen to you, MAKE life happen, grab the opportunities that present themselves and enjoy this wild life because you only get one shot! As creatives, we have wild imaginations, often we are the best at creating scenarios in our head and seeing them play out in minute detail. You need to use this to your advantage, think about what could go right, analyse what the risks are and make sure you're always stepping outside of your comfort zone!

SURROUNDING YOURSELF WITH GO-GETTERS

You are the driving force in the business - we have established this, right? So why does it even matter who you hang about with at the weekend? I've just spent the entire last chapter banging on about the importance of taking control of your own destiny and now I'm dictating who you hang about with? What a cheek, eh?

Well, not really. Everything I have said in the previous chapter is true. The shift starts with you but it doesn't end there. If you're absolutely smashing it at work during the week and then hanging about with jobless stoners at the weekend, I can guarantee you it will start to affect your performance; it's probably affecting your performance now (no offense jobless stoners - you do you, hun). You might think, "ah, but I can keep my work and private life separate, so it's fine". It's not, and you either get on board with it now or you'll realise three years down the line that you should have just got on board with it now... so, er, get on board with it now and safe yourself the hassle.

Am I telling you to delete every lazy person from your life? Of course not! I'm not suggesting you delete your entire Facebook friends list, including family and start all over again but if you are someone who is driven, creative, inspiring, then you need to acknowledge and nurture that aspect of your personality. Not only will it make you feel great, it will come in handy in your time(s) of need.

I am very guarded with my own energy. We have all heard of mood hoovers, right? Those people that can suck the life out of the room just with their presence. That's a real thing btw, it's a palpable energy that usurps all other energies and you want to consider limiting your time around them. Don't be getting the big scissors out and chopping major members of your family and friends list out of your life after reading this chapter, but you absolutely need to look after and respect your own energy. You'll be thinking of a few mood hoovers you know right now. You MIGHT even recognise the victim mentality in them that I was talking about in Chapter 3. Nothing's ever their fault, everything's crap, bad things always happen to them... even writing this is exhausting. So what's the opposite of this and why should we be actively seeking them out?

The opposite of the mood hoover is the positive go-getter (I just spent longer than I care to admit trying to think of something catchy - what's the opposite of a hoover anyway? A pressure washer?!) Have you heard of the saying "You are the sum of the 5 people you spend the most time with"? Who do you spend the most time with right now? Are their life aspirations aligned to yours? Or are you getting the odd snide comment for wanting better for yourself? BEWARE! You need to start consciously surrounding yourself with people that are on the same path or steps ahead of where you want to be. Surrounding yourself with these like-minded people will feel like a tonic for the soul. When people say they've "found their tribe" and you have no idea what they're talking about, you will know when you find your own tribe!

Back in 2016, when I was getting out of the comfort zone by joining the business accelerator programme, one of the biggest unexpected benefits was the other people on there. I'd go as far to say that the success of that programme for me was 90% to do with the amazing people they managed to pull together into the room. You can imagine a bunch of excited, super creative, forward thinking, ambitious, anything-is-possible type business owners all in one room. I think that intake was about 70 or so brand new potential friends and at the time, I had no idea how life changing it would be. It was like networking on an industrial scale. The programme encouraged us to work together, solve each others problems, and share our own experiences in order to propel each other forward, avoiding the mistakes and pitfalls any of us had made in the past. It was like having the fast track airport security pass, except a business version. I was learning from all kinds of different people in there. Inventors, fintech entrepreneurs, ex footballers turned business owners, fitness gurus, fashion designers, drink developers, chefs, psychologists, architects, dog trainers... you name it, they were in there. It was so useful to be pulled out of my own bubble and to see how other people in completely different sectors had overcome adversity, and flourished or failed (just as useful!) in business. Aside from all the problem solving and storytelling, I was inadvertently finding my business pal tribe, some of whom I see once a year, some of whom I see once a week STILL, but most of whom I know I could message at any point and ask for help or advice, as they could with me.

I started spending more and more of my time with these people. Going to lunch, working with them during the day, going out at the weekend and having some of the best years of my life socially. I realised that I had two distinct groups of friends now. One was my best friend group who didn't have a business. And they, quite rightly, were not massively interested in talking about business often, or ever. Which I respect! But when I didn't have my business pals, I still needed to talk about work; I had to get it out of my system! But now, I had my business pals and boy, did we talk about work. 24/7 work chat. Constantly coming up with new ideas and solutions, dreaming up partnerships, sharing resources and sharing the sometimes mammoth weight of being a business owner. It sounds really boring but we were all feeding off each other's energy. We were picking each other up when we needed it the most and with enough energy to go round, it wasn't long before any bad moods were turned on their head. It was absolutely magic!! I actually remember one time when I confessed to my friend Grant that I didn't know if I could do this anymore. Business was hard. I felt like I was running out of options to make it all work and I was exhausted. Later that day, he assembled a business intervention. He said he had never seen me like this and had pulled together some of the brightest brains over a few bottles of wine and we were going to hash everything out and fix it together. Well, needless to say, it worked because as you can tell, I am still here. You need to surround yourself with this safety blanket of people who have your back and will pull you back from the brink when you need it the most because they have been there before themselves.

I'm all for a healthy balance, so I have my non-business pals who are tonic in themselves. I don't talk about work with them, they are a total escape from my day-to-day. And I have my three best business friends who I speak to, well daily to be honest. Louise, Christine and Margaret are my three business besties and I met them all at that accelerator. We totally understand each other, know when one person needs to be picked up, always there with advice and support for each other. Even in the pandemic, when no one was going anywhere, we were out in freezing cold weather walking round a lake just to get some time with each other (Louise was very pregnant and I was terrified she was going to slip!). Finding your tribe is about building your support network. As you and your business grow, you are going to need more support than you could possibly imagine. Sometimes it's as simple as a bit of accountability to get stuff done, or a kick up the arse when you're repeating the same damaging habits, other times it's a full blown intervention that needs staged but you need to get looking for these golden folks!

Where to find them? If you're reading this right now at the start of your business tribe building journey, it might seem a bit overwhelming. The first step is to get yourself to a local business networking event. They exist online and in person but I would suggest going to an in person one. If the idea of walking into a room of people on your own terrifies you, good. That's your comfort zone trying to keep you cosy - step out of the cosy! Networking events never get any easier btw - I still don't like that first 10 minutes, especially if I'm already going in there with an imposter syndrome mindset. The first thing to remember is everyone is actually in the same boat. It's not in our nature to love walking into a room of people we don't know and trying to strike up a conversation. Head for the tea station first, take your time making a cup of tea, chat to the next person who comes over to make themselves a cup of tea. They might have just entered the room too. Show a real interest in them and what they do. As soon as you get that first conversation out of the way, you will start feeling much better. It's ok to be nervous. It's also ok to tell people it's your first networking event and you're nervous. Being vulnerable (and honest) isn't a weakness and often it makes people warm to you. Eventually, you will become a networking pro and you will recognise that nervousness in other people. Then it's your job to pull them into your circle and reassure them. You never know who they are, they could be your new business bestie!

Next, I would start looking for a suitable business collective to join. This could be a group for creative businesses who all meet once a month, or an online group where you can forge meaningful relationships. Or it can of course, be one of the more intense business accelerators, like the one I joined. Some of these will be free but the better ones will have a cost (which is a tax deductible business expense remember!). Be aware you don't accidentally join a bro club pyramid scheme! I can't actually name these because I will 100% get sued, but if someone is being very intense trying to get you to sign up to something, I would be asking questions about what's in it for them. Some of these groups work on a "you must introduce x amount of new people every month" and you "must attend or send someone in your place". I'm sure they work for some people but if I am paying for a membership, I want to be able to miss some sessions to run my business without having to send my mum in to fill my seat! Make sure whatever you're joining works for you, adds value to you as a business owner and doesn't impede your ability to run and grow your business.

If you're looking for an accelerator or a group programme, I would first be asking your local government if they have any business programmes or training you can get involved in. In Scotland the support is pretty good. Wherever you live, it's generally in your Governments best interest to nurture new business owners because ultimately, you have the potential to create jobs, pay chunky tax bills and they should want to help you get there. Secondly, tap into your new network of business friends and see if they know about anything you could join.

Eventually, your brain becomes programmed to make contacts and connections in everything you do. For example,

I have bought and joined countless online training courses for all kinds of things. Often, these courses have Facebook groups as part of the package, to allow you to get to know the other people on the course and ask the course leaders questions. This is a great place to make business friends in the online space without being hindered by where you or they physically live.

Finally, when you're ready to bring out the big guns, you can start looking at business masterminds. Now be aware, these are not cheap and nor should they be. A mastermind is a collective of business owners, normally within a certain turnover bracket, who are paying to be in the room with similarly ambitious business owners. There will likely be events, even trips abroad together, to enable you to forge meaningful business and social relationships with each other. Some people get masterminds mixed up with some sort of year-long business course - it's not that. I saw it as paying to get in the room with other people who were smashing it in business. In late 2020, I was made aware of a government run programme designed to help female business owners and leaders pull themselves out of the covid-shaped hole. I mean, they didn't advertise it as that, but I think that's what it was. There were certain requirements for applying for this. One was turnover based, which I didn't quite qualify for, one was employee numbers, which I was JUST under as well, and the other one was being a women - TICK! Before I applied, I had actually just read an article about the difference between men and women when applying for jobs. It said that men were WAY (sorry I can't find the %) more likely to apply for a job even if they didn't actually fit all the criteria, whereas women were more likely to need to tick all the criteria boxes before considering themselves able to go for the job. I think when I read that, I decided to stop taking those criteria so literally, so I just applied for this business group. Because I didn't fit the criteria really, I didn't expect to get in. I REALLY wanted to get in though because I needed to get in the room with people who were smashing it business-wise, compared to me. When I was actually accepted, I realised we were all at a fairly similar level. The programme was great but it cemented the idea in my head that if I wanted to make millions, I had to hang about with millionaires - cue paying £15k for my first mastermind experience! The mastermind was jam-packed with great content, had monthly trainings and access to some pretty high profile people. But again, it always comes down to the people for me. I was paying to get access to the go-getters and game-changers. I would never meet these people normally, they have skills and experience I could only dream of and now, I know I could call most of them my friends. I should also add that a big part of life for me is the social side, so now, I have business pals who enjoy drinking wine as much as me pretty much all over the globe. £15k well spent!

I know the world of masterminds is an absolute nightmare... if you can even find any. So I will constantly keep my mastermind page on my website updated for you and you can always drop me a message if you want to chat about them;

www.jennydrew.com

I really can't stress how important it is to build your network. I believe the network I have is the reason I am still in business. The amount of times I have been pulled from the brink by these people, inspired by them, or joined forces with them to create something amazing. If you only do one thing today take the first step to growing that network. Join a group or book an event. I promise you, you won't regret it!

ASKING FOR HELP - HOW AND WHO?

When I first started in business, I was pretty young at 24. I had no experience of business, I had never had a "real" job in the sense that it had all been retail type jobs before, with no responsibility as such. I was as green as you like and I had my own ideas of how I had to build this business. I thought I needed to build it alone. With no help from anyone, financially or otherwise. Zero help. I'm going to put it down to naivety, lack of world experience or absolute stupidity because I can categorically tell you now that it's the wrong way to go about it!

I really had something to prove back then - maybe I still do now but for different reasons! I was in survival mode. The recession had made finding a job a bloody nightmare, so I had to make my own job in the form of a business. I felt hard done by, I was in that victim state. I had a bit of an 'eff you world' mentality and I wanted to show everyone what I was capable of, alone. I had it in my head that if anyone really helped me, they would own a chunk of my success and I couldn't stand up and, hand on heart, say I had done this on my own. I also see this in other young entrepreneurs who have a bone to pick with the world. Let me tell you right now, it's not the way to go about it. Get help from EVERYONE.

The fact you are reading this book must mean that you've already realised that learning from other people's mistakes and experiences is the way to get ahead. Why make the same mistakes as those who have gone before you if you can avoid it? That's not progress, that's absolute madness. But who should you ask? What help is reasonable? And how do you avoid pissing people off in the process? I have a system for this, based around being very aware that actually no one owes you anything, people are bloody busy and their time is very precious - It's called the NNNEAR System.

NEED

NETWORK

NURTURE

EXCHANGE

ADVERTISE

RECIPROCATE

NEED - What do you actually need? If you don't know what you need, you'll never be able to really find the right people to help you. I'm not talking about money here btw, I'm talking about knowledge, skills, people, networks. Perhaps you don't have a strategy in place for where the business is going for the next 5 years, so there's no real direction in your business. In that case, you need to find someone who has the skills, knowledge and experience of building great business strategies. Let's use this as an example moving forward. Once you know what you need, you turn to your Network.

NETWORK - Chapter 4 was all about building your network, now it's time to start using it for more than a night out with adopted colleagues. Who have you met recently who either helps other businesses build strategies or seems to really have their shit together themselves - so must either be amazing at planning or knows someone who is? What organisations exist that can help you? Again, I'll always go down the government help path as they quite often have people who can help you or grants that can pay people to help you. If no one immediately comes to mind, I'll often post on social media telling people I'm looking for a bit of advice with X, Y and Z. You'll usually find someone who is willing to help you out, or a recommendation of someone you should connect with. Which leads me nicely onto the next step in the system, Nurture.

NURTURE - Nurturing the relationship between you and whoever is going to help you is crucial. Whether this is an individual or an organisation, you need to nurture it to ensure you get the help you need. Yes, people want to help, but people also want their time to be valued. A lot of business owners will give their time for free to select people but only if they know that you won't rip the piss and that you'll actually go and action what they teach you. So start grafting, be grateful, and prove to them that you're worth their time, which should hopefully result in the Exchange part of the system.

EXCHANGE - If you're doing everything right, you'll soon come to the Exchange stage. This is where the business or individual agrees to help you out. Make it as easy as possible for them. Don't ask them to travel to you, make sure you buy the coffee, don't, for God's sake, be late and don't keep them longer than you agreed. Be super grateful, tell them how much you appreciate their time and that you'll let them know how you get on. In the best scenarios, you might really hit it off with the person and they become a permanent fixture in your network but that's not always necessary for you to get some of the initial guidance that you're looking for. Is there something you can offer them in return? For example, when a business friend of mine, Carol Deveney, who is an expert in helping small businesses understand the corporate world, offered to spend a whole day with me, helping with project management, I said I would get her dressmaking. From chatting to her, I knew she wanted something non-work related to spend her time on - a self confessed work-aholic - and she quite fancied learning to sew and loved clothes, so I vowed to get her dressmaking regardless of how many classes that would take. It was the perfect exchange! If you don't have a dream exchange scenario like Carol and I, then sometimes simply shouting about this person and their services on your social media and in your networks is a good exchange. Remember here that regardless of where you are in business, everyone has something to offer someone else. No one has your particular set of skills and you might be surprised what you can do for someone who may seem miles ahead of you in business! Value yourself!

ADVERTISE - If the person that helped you is a professional then ask them where you can leave a review. Even if you didn't pay for the services, you can still write a sparkling review about the advice and service you received. You can talk about them on social media and tag them to expose them to your audience and you can bear them in mind if you ever know anyone who needs their services in the future.

RECIPROCATE - Then it's time to give back. Not to the person who helped you but to someone who is in need of your help. They might not present themselves immediately but be open to sharing your knowledge and experience with earlier stage entrepreneurs. Giving back in this way is good karma/vibes/energy and will make you feel good and more likely to ask for help again in the future (because you know you'll reciprocate the goodwill with someone else and so the cycle continues).

Dealing with individuals who can help you, or government organisations, require this same approach. Over the years, I have seen people approach the government organisations we have here in Scotland with a real sense of entitlement. "They're government funded so they have to help me", err, no they don't! Yes, they are government funded and officially, they are supposed to help everyone, but these organisations are run by human beings who will decide very early on whether they like you or not and whether they want to go right out of their way to help you. Don't get me wrong, you won't see that last sentence printed on official government pamphlets but I know it to be true because I've seen people get the absolute bare minimum of help because they had an entitled attitude and I've seen people get unimaginable amounts of help and assistance because they were gracious, grateful and took the time to build real relationships with the gatekeepers of the funds! The moral of this story is don't be a dick, really!

Here's a wee example of a time when I have used this method to my advantage. Back in the pre-franchise days, I could not have been more clueless. I didn't know anyone who had built a franchise really and despite going to lots of networking events, I was finding that franchisors in Scotland are few and far between! This, to be fair, made me even more determined to build the franchise because I knew if it was this hard, most people wouldn't do it, wiping out a ton of potential competition from the get go (at time of writing, I still have no direct competitors in franchising)! I turned to my business accelerator network and asked if anyone could help. It turned out there was an up-and-coming franchise company in the Glasgow hub that I was in but I hadn't met them yet! I was put in touch with my now friend, Stephen, who was only too happy to have a coffee with me. Over the next few years, he gave me loads of guidance from how to recruit franchises to how to find property, and everything in between. He has undeniably helped me more than I have helped him but on top of telling everyone that would listen about his company, I did help him recruit a key member of staff a few years ago. He was looking for a senior manager and I just so happened to know someone who fitted the bill perfectly, was interested in his company and was low-key looking for a new job. I was so delighted to be able to help him, since he had given so much of his time and knowledge to me! Since then, I have had a few people come to me asking for help with potentially franchising their business and I have spoken publicly about my franchising experience in the hope it encourages more Scottish businesses to consider it as a method of growth. I will continue to do this and help small business where I can as I feel, with all the help I have had over my time in business, I really owe it to the business community to share my skills. I suppose this book is a bit of that as well. If it helps one person realise their potential, then it has done its job!

Need: Franchise help

Network: Espark

Nurture: met for a coffee

Exchange: helped me loads with my ops manual

Advertise: a job they had and found them an employee

Reciprocate: I have since spoken on a 121 basis and publicly about franchising

If you are the kind of person who enjoys meeting new people and making new friends then you should consider this chapter the key to your business super power. Recently, whilst chatting with my fellow masterminders Louise, Christine and Margaret, I discovered that contrary to being the norm, my love of meeting new people was actually putting me in the minority. We were talking about masterminds and why you would join them. The mastermind I have with these three fabulous ladies had a very unique, organic creation. We met in the business accelerator I spoke about previously, stayed in touch and YEARS later, realised the power in our tiny support network. However there are larger masterminds you can pay to join which are arguably much, much easier to get involved with (I think the planets really aligned when I met those three!), such as the year long one I joined in 2021. We were talking about what we were all personally drawn to about a particular mastermind, how long we would want it to be, what we would want included and we realised our wants and needs were all vastly different (also our strength as a foursome of course!). I'm here for the connection, all day long. I love meeting new people, without even meaning it, every time someone introduces themselves to me, my brain whirrs into action trying to figure out how we could work together, how we could help each other or who in my network needs to meet this person. At some point, I had to work at this and like anything else, it eventually becomes second nature, but if you are already a social butterfly then embrace this superpower! I actually attribute a lot of my success in business to genuinely enjoying building meaningful relationships with fellow business owners. I also, without doubt, attribute this to the enjoyment I have had along the way. If you have a job, you should enjoy it or do something else. If you have a business, you should absolutely love it and use it to embrace experiences and opportunities that create a life (including social life!) you absolutely love.

One caveat to the above that I have only learned recently is, some people won't like you and there's no amount of charisma or charm that will change their mind, and nor should it. I really struggled with this actually and I think it's because I was able to fit into a room of Scottish folk, no bother. There's a banter between people who live in the same place as you but even moving into a UK wide space or a world wide space, I discovered the banter isn't universal, and some of them can't even understand my accent. It caused issues. I thought "oh great, I've finally found a room I'm not welcome in". I soon discovered that a lot of them were feeling the same. And it wasn't that anyone wasn't welcome; it was nerves, egos and competitive alpha personalities (my own included!) causing this unusual atmosphere. It was another lesson for me as, if I want to be in these rooms - which I do - then I need to learn that the aim of the game isn't to make everyone like you. Put the jester costume away, Jenny, you're not the hired entertainment! The aim of the game is to find the 10% in that room who you really gel with, whilst staying open to the other 90%. Give yourself permission to trust your gut with people - if it feels off, it probably is. Don't waste time and energy on people who don't think you are their kettle of fish - chances are, they aren't yours either. Who wants a bloody kettle of fish anyway?! Overrated!

OUTSOURCING WHAT YOUR NOT GOOD AT

Before I start this chapter I want to give your permission to skip it and come back to it later. The reason for that is we're about to GO DEEP into your finances and if you're not in the zone for it I'm allowing you to skip it if you promise to come back to it. This chapter is so important for the growth of your business but I have lost count of the amount of books that I have put down and never revisited because of a heavy chapter right in the middle that I couldn't deal with at the time. The rest of this book will still make sense even if you read this chapter last. But I mean it, you NEED to come back to it and get this stuff sorted, ok? OK, let's do this.

Hands up if you started a business to work harder and longer than you did with a job and on projects/task you don't enjoy? Oh, no one? But I bet there is a long list of things you have ended up doing that you dread every day, or are so crap at that it takes you forever? Am I right? What if I told you that you should be outsourcing or getting someone else to do these jobs so you can make more money? Now, I know what you're thinking - you can't afford to outsource anything and it's cheaper to do it all yourself. If you resonate with this, you are stifling your company's growth and you will work yourself into the ground to the point where you don't even want a business anymore. Hopefully, by the end of this chapter I will have turned your outsourcing mindset on its head!

In the very early stages of business, it's really common to do everything yourself. And without a ton of start up cash, it's just the way it has to be. But after a year has passed, you need to figure out whether your business is sustainable; if you're working for nothing, - we've got a problem! If you're currently flying solo in business, there's an easy 2-step formula for working out whether you can afford to hire some help.

Step 1 - Hourly Rate

Let's figure out how much money you bring into the company per hour of work. Take a week and create a diary documenting how much you're working (and what you're working on). This should include hours actually doing the work but also the odd 15 minutes here and there when you've decided to reply to an email outside of work… that counts as work too. Let's say you work 50 hours per week on average. Work out how many weeks of holiday you're likely to take a year - let's say 4. That means, as you work 48 weeks per year at 50 hours per week, you work 2,400 hours per year. Now let's say your company turns over 70k a year - 70,000 divided by 2,400 is £29 p/h. I should state at this point, this is not how you work out what you should be charging clients if you do 121 work, that's a different story entirely. This is how much money you bring into the company per hour of work.

Step 2 - What's in your profit pot?

You might never have worked this out. You could be running your business on a wing and a prayer like I was in the early days. I used to look at my business bank accounts and if there was a certain figure in there, I was content and thought I was doing really well. I can tell you now this is a terrible way to run a business but don't feel bad if this is resonating with you because you don't know what you don't know... and soon you **will** know what I know - because I'm going to tell you!

You don't need an accountant to figure out whether you are profitable or not, you need a calculator and information about every outgoing your business has vs your income. Let's look at last month. Write down all your outgoings, bills you paid, books you bought, coffees with clients you paid for, stock you purchased, wages you paid to yourself - everything. Write it all down (or even better, stick it in a spreadsheet) and tally it up. Now look at all your income from last month, invoices that were paid to you, products you sold, courses that were purchased from you - everything! Now take your outgoings away from your income and you have your profit for that month (Let's call it our profit pot because I'm visual and it helps!). There will be accountants squirming in their seats right now but getting a very basic grasp on these figures is better than no grasp at all, right?

That will give you an idea of your profit from that month. But of course, we really need to look at this picture for a whole year. There are some months we make a loss in business because we have, for example, bought a lot of stock, or taken on a new premises, but when we look at the figures for the year as a whole it's a much healthier and profitable outlook so you can't really judge your whole business by one month. I know it's a laborious task but trust me, you need to get a handle on this to be able to outsource, grow and feel in control of your business finances. If you have an accountant, you can pull a profit and loss account from your accounting software and it will tell you at the top what your turnover is and at the very bottom what your net profit is. That's your profit pot, a percentage of which we can use for outsourcing!

Aside from outsourcing, you really need to know your numbers to be able to make sensible decisions within your business. There is a saying: "turnover is vanity, net profit is sanity" and that's because you'll get people boasting about their million pound turnover but neglecting to mention that their costs are 1.5 million. I see online people talking about their 3/4/5/6/7-figure businesses but really the congratulations should be in the profit because that's the true sign of a businesses health and success.

If you're currently not in profit, I would be cagey about outsourcing anything until you get a handle on where you are losing money. A consistent loss-making business is only going to end one way, so it's time for radical action, and some serious conversations with yourself about what needs to change moving forward.

Don't feel down about discovering this, feel happy that you're figuring it out at this early stage and now you can do something about it. So many people spend every waking hour on a business that isn't profitable enough to serve them. You didn't start this business to work like mad for the rest of your life so let's see what can be done to fix it now before you're absolutely scunnered!

If you are profitable but do the calculation above and figure out you're working for £3.50 an hour, then we need to consider why this is the case. Are you working 70 hours a week? That's too much and you will burn out and then be no use to anyone - I've seen it happen. Do you need to make more money? Where can we increase prices, or increase units of sales without increasing the hours spent in the business?

Let's look at your prices first of all. Are you charging enough? I speak to people every week who are undercharging for their products/services because "people won't pay that", but let's remember that Tiffany's sell a big gold paperclip for $1,500 so if you're in the right market, people will actually pay anything. More about pricing in Chapter 10. Upping your prices is the easiest way to increase your profit margins (and hourly rate).

Secondly, what else could you add into your offering or upsell to your customers that offers them great value but doesn't take up too much of your time. Let's say you are a dog behaviourist and you work one-on-one with dog owners who need help training their pet. Could you also upsell them a PDF e-book on common behavioural issues when out on a walk and how to tackle them? This could be a small fee, but you only have to write it once and then it's a digital product you can sell as an extra to every single new customer, with very little of your time taken up. You could also consider having gold, silver and bronze packages. So when a new customer enquires about your service you have the ability to sell them more advanced packages that offer them more value and make you more money. Extra value isn't always necessarily your time one-on-one. It could be that the top package gives them access to your VIP Facebook group for dog owners, where they can support each other and get some access to you and your knowledge. Try and think outside the box. What are other people in your industry not doing? Why not? That could be the thing you end up doing that really sets you apart from them. It's a mistake to look at what your competitors are doing and ONLY do those things - that's not competition! Just because they are more established or appear to be more successful doesn't mean they are doing everything right. In some cases, existing businesses are so stuck in their ways that there is a real opportunity to come in, do things differently and shake up the market to your advantage.

Do you have a one-and-done business model? Do your customers come to you once and rarely come back? Is that the nature of your business in that the service you offer is only really needed once? If that's the case, you need to either add other complementary services to keep them engaged with your business or you need to offer some sort of incentive for them to tell people they know about you. I don't think there are many businesses that couldn't find a way to create repeat custom. It is MUCH easier to sell to someone who already knows and trusts you than it is to get a brand new customer, so finding a way to bring those customers back to you is so important.

Once you start to increase the money you're bringing in without increasing the hours you're working (maybe even decreasing those hours, if you're working like mad?!) then you can start to think about what can be outsourced! There - we got there in the end!

Write down all the business related tasks you do on a monthly basis. For example:

Bookkeeping

Packaging orders

Updating stock on the website

Writing a blog for the website

Daily social media

Responding to emails from customers

Paying invoices

Teaching classes

Making up class kits

New class/product development

Buying stock

Now you want to work out roughly how many hours a month you are working on these tasks. You can estimate some but I do recommend logging your tasks for a week to figure out what the split is.

Put a mark beside all the tasks that only you can do. For example you might be the only person who can pay invoices because you are the only person who has access to the bank accounts (and you want it to stay that way). These are things you are currently unwilling to outsource.

Put a wee happy face beside the things you enjoy and a wee sad face next to the things you hate doing.

Let's say it looks like this now:

Bookkeeping and accounting - 5 hours : (

Packaging orders - 33 hours : (

Updating stock on the website - 13 hours

Writing a blog for the website - 3 hours :)

Daily social media - 65 hours

Responding to emails from customers - 30 hours : (

Paying invoices - 2 hours (not to be outsourced)

Teaching classes – 53 hours :)

Making up class kits -12 hours : (

New class/product development - 5 hours :)

Buying stock - 5 hours :)

My definition of outsourcing is giving tasks away to people or programs so that I do not have to do them, so I include hiring employees in this "outsourcing" bracket because they take tasks off my plate. Let's start with bookkeeping. Very few enjoy this, especially in the creative world I live in. It was one of the very first things I outsourced. Your options here are to look for software that makes your life easier and turns that 5 hours into 3 hours, hiring a member of staff to do it as part of their job, or outsourcing to an external company or freelancer. The aim here is to either find a way to decrease the time you need to spend on it, or hire someone who will do it quicker and cost you less than your own hourly rate would (that you worked out earlier!). I also always check that there is enough money in the profit pot to cover this with plenty left over for cash flow (more about cash flow later!)!

In our earlier example we worked out that our hourly rate was £29 per hour. So essentially, bookkeeping is costing us £145 per month because you are spending 5 hours of your time on tasks that are, of course, necessary for a business but are non income generating. Let's say you subscribe to a piece of software that costs £20 per month but means you are now only spending 3 hours on bookkeeping. You have essentially made a saving of £38 AND have 2 extra hours than can be put to income generating tasks (5 hours - 3 hours = 2 hours. 2 hours x £29 - £20 software fee = £38). **As long as there is**

enough money in the profit pot to cover this additional monthly fee then this is a win!

Another option would be to outsource it all completely. Perhaps you can get an accountant to do your bookkeeping and accounting for £70 a month. You suspect there will still be an hour a month of admin that you will need to do so it's saving you 4 hours of time every month. The saving here is £75 plus 4 hours that you can use on income generating tasks! Again, as long as you've got it spare in the profit pot, it's a good idea!

The thing about outsourcing is it takes things off your plate that are potentially holding you back. So, apart from the cold hard finances of you wasting your precious billed hours on things you don't like, it actually affects the rest of your working life.

Let's talk about cash flow. You will have heard the saying "cash is king", right? It's true because without it, you're in trouble. It doesn't matter how much money you have locked up in machinery or money coming in for orders 2 months down the line, if you don't have cash right now, you could go bust tomorrow. It's one of the main reasons small companies fail and it's entirely avoidable! Because you worked out your income and outgoing earlier, the cash flow task is almost done for you. Cash flow forecasts are about looking to the future. You'll know that every month your internet costs £X, rent cost £Y and your insurance cost £Z. If you have been trading for a year or so, you'll also have an idea of what you can expect to come in in sales every month, perhaps with a %

increase on last year's sales. You might even be able to look ahead to the next 12 months and know what months you're likely to make more, especially if there is any seasonality to your business. If you add all your outgoings each month and all your estimated income into the cash flow sheet, you will be able to confidently see whether you're likely to dive, survive or thrive over the next 12 months. In here, you can also add in outgoings in the form of anything you want to outsource and you'll be able to see if you will be able to afford that for the next 12 months. This should give you the confidence to know whether or not you can truly afford to pay for someone else to work with you.

This all might sound like a lot of work but these are the tools that will help you grow, mitigating your risks as you go. I wish someone had sat me down in the early days and told me how these tools weren't just models they stick in textbooks at university so they have something to test you on at the end of term (oooooh, burn!), but they are actually useful working models for the early business owners. I happen to know that MOST early business owners don't use these tools, either because they don't think they apply to them or because they're too busy grafting doing the work that brings in the money. At some point, you need to figure out a way to step away from the graft and carve out some time every week for growth orientated work like I've told you about in this chapter. The good thing about barely anyone else in your current situation doing this is you, my friend, just got the upper hand. By reading and implementing this chapter you're at least one step ahead of your similar stage competition. And if that isn't enough to make you run to my website, download all the tools and re-read this chapter, then maybe nothing will! STOP PLAYING SMALL and start working smart!

Tools are over on the website;

www.jennydrew.com/bookbonus

LEARNING & IMPLEMENTING

I could talk about learning and implementing UNTIL THOSE PROVERBIAL COWS WALK THROUGH THAT GATE, because I am so passionate about getting this message across. Learning is a crucial part of your business growth story and I see education coming from two sources: internal and external.

Internal Education

Internal learning comes from you as a direct result of your actions and is one of the most effortless ways to absorb information. Let's say, for example, you sell a digital product to someone without any terms and conditions. Ten days later, they come back and want a refund despite the digital product being delivered already and them having no way to actually return it. You don't have any terms and conditions, so they didn't actually agree to anything and you have no option but to refund them. I can bet the first thing you'll do is get yourself some watertight terms and conditions because you don't want to find yourself in that situation again. This is essentially learning from your mistakes and it's easy because it's not a hypothetical situation; it's already happened to you and you have emotions attached to it.

External Education

External learning is just about everything else that happens outside of you. Let's use the example from above and say three months ago, you went to a legal seminar for small businesses. You sat there for an hour but actually, you started zoning out about 10 minutes in (sorry lawyers of the world, this will be ringing true for a lot of my creative business pals though, AM I RIGHT?). You took some notes, one of which was "terms and conditions are important" and then you shut that notepad never to be revisited again. Now three months ago someone told you that your terms and conditions were important. It piqued your interest enough for you to even write it down. But it didn't seem important or exciting enough for you to do anything about it. Only three months later when, in practice, you were on the receiving end of the negative effects of NOT having any terms and conditions, were you shoved into action because suddenly it wasn't theoretical - it was real!

Other types of external education would include the traditional routes like university, books, online courses, one-off seminars, online blogs, educational videos and less traditional, like social media and apps!

You can learn literally anything you like now, information is absolutely everywhere and often for free. So if we have all this information at our fingertips for free, why are we not all absolutely killing it in our chosen field? Why are we still paying for courses and books? Why did you buy this book? Actually, the problem lies in the absolute abundance and overwhelm of the situation we have now. What a brat I am to complain about the wealth of information available to us but it's being misused every day! I remember when I was young, we were lucky enough to have a PC in the house (we're going back to when that was something you considered lucky, not the norm) and we did have the internet too, but it wasn't a patch on what it is now and it was expensive (like 10p a minute expensive!!). We had a program for the computer called Encartra - do you remember this? It was basically a kind of interactive offline encyclopedia for your PC and I loved it. It had videos, a search bar, illustrations, sound bites - it kept me entertained for hours and it helped with my homework! The only other option of its kind though was an actual encyclopedia or a book but I remember thinking this search bar was the future! Now the search bar WAS the future, but so was falling into 3-hour long wild goose chase wormholes and coming out the other side confused and with more questions than answers. I believe today the biggest issue we have is too much of a good thing, which kills our focus and overwhelms our brain. In my case, when I am overwhelmed or stressed by a situation, I go to sleep - which you can imagine isn't the best for productivity! It still happens to me now - if I'm under a lot of stress at work, I need to nap to give my brain a break (and probably let it find the answer to my problems in my subconscious!).

How do we make the most of this plethora of information without getting overwhelmed? You IMPLEMENT IT.

Implementation is the difference between success and failure. But implementation isn't easy. It takes dedication, time and focus to stay on the path. Coming from someone who's personality means I am the opposite of a completer-finisher, I can tell you this ain't easy, but the rewards at the end are sweet, my friend!

It can be easy to get stuck in the continuous learning cycle. I'll go and do this course on SEO then I'm going to do this course on copywriting then I'm going to do this course on product photography, then I'm going to do this course on colour theory… does this sound familiar? Some people get stuck in this cycle with actual university/college courses, for some it's constant self-help books, other's it's often expensive online courses, one after the other. You need to stop and ask yourself what have you learned, then implemented recently? Before you start a new course you need to ask yourself "Am I going to implement this afterwards?". If the answer to these questions is "nothing" and "no", then you are stuck in a vicious cycle of learning. Yes, you're going to be great in a pub quiz, you'll be an amazing business course encyclopedia for every business pal you know, but you're letting yourself down because you're not using your knowledge and skill to better yourself.

Let's look at why you might be stuck in this vicious cycle. It's usually fear based. We are all capable of learning. You do the course, write the notes, do the workbooks, finish the course and you feel a sense of accomplishment because you finished something. Everything you learn has a high chance of having the predictable and safe outcome and it feels good! We are designed to do more of what feels good. However, if you need to take what you have learned, apply it to the real world, implement it in your business, take the theory and test it out - well now we are into scary territory. We're out of the comfort zone, we can't predict the outcome, we might lose money, or customers, or we might look stupid! Your body is telling you to retreat, it's not safe out there, you might get eaten by a lion... well, no you won't (unless you run a safari park, maybe don't take too many risks there!).

All of this is from my own past experiences and looking back,— I can see times when I did not want to get out of that comfort zone. But we know that's where the magic happens, that's where the growth is and that's where you need to be prepared to go in order to Stop Playing Small!

Moving forward this is how we are rolling - Learn > Implement > Repeat. Could be a Fatboy Slim song. Your learning should be a mixture of internal and external learning. It might sound simple but you have no idea how many people do not do this! I also recently heard this constant learning being referred to as self-sabotage and I couldn't agree more.

An example of the Learn > Implement > Repeat could be:

You find an online course about making money through Facebook groups (external education).

You decide whether you actually need this course or if you are procrastinating, avoiding something else that you SHOULD be doing.

You commit to completing the course and then allow yourself a set amount of time after the course to implement it.

You then allow time after implementation to learn from your own experiences/mistakes (internal education).

You tweak your original learnings and implement the new ones.

Only once you've implemented something can you consider learning something new.

Seems pretty simple right? Well, it's not and that's because today's world is designed to pull us in several different directions. Marketing is such that you might feel that you're on a conveyor belt of education, just trying to better yourself without actually getting anywhere.

I think I was caught in this cycle myself for about a year. I kept joining short business courses, spending my valuable time joining them, completing them and realising at the end that I was no further forward. In some cases, I didn't even qualify for the course and had to fight to get on them (with government funded ones you sometimes need to have a certain turnover or certain number of staff), thinking THIS course would be the game changer. This is when I realised two things:

1. Education is completely useless without adequate time and the will to implement the learnings;
2. I personally don't value things unless I pay for them, which will also be the case for a lot of you!

The second part is vital and it will be different for many people but as someone who has made a business out of selling courses, I actually see the "I don't value things unless I pay for them" playing out with my own customers in their leisure learning, so it may well be the same for you. Shortly after this realisation, I paid a chunk of money, as you know, to join a mastermind and it's the easiest money I have ever spent. As a pretty risk averse business owner, the ease with which I paid this even surprised me, but it felt right. It was as if a lightbulb had gone off in my brain and I knew to take my business to the next level I had to have real skin in the game. I would never allow myself to waste £15k of the company's money so the only option was to learn, implement and cash out! And that's exactly what I did.

About four months into this mastermind, I had used the network and the teachings within it and I had implemented those teachings to the letter - I'm not ashamed to say it was a great struggle, but I was dedicated to the end result, which was almost four times my initial investment just four months in - not bad, eh.

Find your motivator!

I have found myself in this struggle, trying to see something out to the end. I remember battling with my own need for variety at times. One time, I was in implementation mode, writing the launch of a new online course. Like I said before, I am not a completer-finisher, I am a magpie of the highest order. I find everything interesting except what I'm doing at times, and it was an internal battle between what I KNEW I had to do to succeed and what I wanted to do to feel good. Part of the struggle for me was around what felt like a metric ton of emails that had to be written before I launched a brand new course. I don't mind writing at all, but the list of emails I had to write was almost never-ending and I was finding it so hard to concentrate and not get distracted. I actually decided I had to start rewarding myself with something after every 3 emails written. I would get up, have a cup of tea and a wee chocolate as a well done and an energy boost. Honestly, I was like a dog rewarding myself with a treat but it worked! And as I got closer to the end of that list, it got easier and easier to keep going. I consider myself to be highly self-motivated but even I was struggling big time with this. I also think, looking back, there was an element of self-sabotage. I was working towards the biggest product launch of my life, my goals were big and I was almost scared that it would work, which sounds weird but there was definitely some sort of fear at play here. I was able to push the tempting procrastination and the fear to one side though by remembering what my motivators are and keeping them in my mind. I suggest, when you find yourself in this situation, you do some work on why you are doing it - what's your motivation for doing what you do? Remembering this is a bit like cheering yourself on in a race - it perks you up and gives you the energy and strength to keep going. For me, I am motivated by growth. Personal growth and business growth. I love achieving things - especially when I know most people think I can't. In fact, one of the best things you can ever do for me is tell me you don't think I can do it, just ask Mr. Millar from my Maths class who thought I wouldn't get anywhere without higher maths, eh! Figuring out your motivation can be a great way to remind yourself of why you're doing what you're doing when you're having a tough day. Your motivator could be your family, a better life, social kudos, proving to yourself you can do it, a lovely handbag*, a fancy car... I'm certainly not judging! But figure it out and use it when you're having a tough day!

The golden rule for learning is making sure you plan to implement, otherwise what's the point?! I don't buy anything (including business books!) or join anything unless I have the time, the will, and the need to implement it at the end. I have seen people become continuous learners in business because it means they never have the chance to actually fail... but they also never have the chance to succeed. Much better to have tried and failed than never tried at all, who said that again? Or was it about love? I don't know but it's true. There is NO shame in failing, it's to be commended if you can use it as internal learning and keep tweaking your model until you strike gold!

*definitely bought myself a Louis Vuitton Handbag as a well done present after this launch!

GRATITUDE FOR YOUR BLESSINGS

It feels incredibly apt that I am writing this chapter on a flight to LA from Heathrow in business class within a private pod, with enough legroom for two of me, and a seat that turns into a bed. I also have a cocktail from their cocktail menu (!!).

This isn't my normal life though. This is the first time I have ever flown business class - the flight attendant can definitely tell by my face and the fact I am videoing everything and I don't care (neither does he!). I am PINCHING myself. I'm sending my husband videos of the menu, I have now lost count of how many WhatsApp's I have sent of me opening and closing my wee pod door. I just can't believe I'm here... but at the same time, I can. I remember 10 years ago, having a friend who often flew business class with work and thinking "that will be me one day", and here we are, made it at last!

Let's rewind to 10 years ago. I was at the start of my business journey. I started the business because I needed income to pay my rent but deep down, I always knew there was so much potential out there. At uni, a few years prior, I had argued tooth and nail with my university about changing the "work experience" module of my Fashion Business Bachelor's degree to an entrepreneurship one. Along with my uni friend and fellow business owner Alissa, we managed to convince the faculty that it would actually be worthwhile for people doing our degree to learn how to run a small business rather than go and work in Topshop on the shop floor. They begrudgingly let Alissa and I run a small enterprise instead of doing work experience. Interestingly, I see they now have entrepreneurship modules in that course so maybe we were just ahead of the curve, but it was cementing in me this desire to be my own boss, even if it wasn't the easiest path.

So many people assume that when you start a business like mine it's going to be a "lifestyle business". First of all, I have a real issue with this because whether you aim to turnover £12k a year or £12 million, a business is hard work. And it seems the term "lifestyle business" is mostly attributed to female owned companies - I have an even bigger issue with that, as if the norm is to assume that female owned businesses should be assumed "lifestyle" until proven otherwise. How condescending. I never intended to own a lifestyle business. I knew I had the capability to create something amazing and sizeable. Not just for me but for my franchisees and my staff. 10 years later, I can say, finally, I feel like people are realising I wasn't messing around.

I'm telling you this because whilst I do believe in the law of attraction and the power of gratitude, I also never sat around waiting for things to happen. There's always been a need for a bit of gentle pressure in order for me to carve this path and get to where I am now, and if you're a female in a creative industry, you need to be prepared to push even harder.

Gratitude itself isn't a new concept. Gratitude, and the things it can do for you in business, I feel, is pretty current. I was fortunate enough to be introduced to this concept by my friend and ex-employer, Soni (I mentioned this back in Chapter 1). I was going through a bit of a rough time with family stuff when I worked for Soni. Him and his partner Sam are two of the most amazing people you could ever meet. They ooze calm; their presence alone chills you out. I had been working for another company when they were considering buying Soni and Sam's business. So they sent me to their gift shop to work prior to the buy out, in order for them to have a known member of staff there who knows how both companies work. I moved over there, and then the deal fell through, but everything happens for a reason, right? Looking back, I was getting daily coaching sessions from Soni.

He was introducing me to a way of thinking I had never come across. He would say things like "when you get angry, it only affects you". How simple, yet how insightful. He encouraged me to say sorry to people who had upset me in my head (for my wrongdoings in a past life and sometimes, in this one) and to forgive them. Now either this makes a lot of sense or you think it's bonkers, either way, I can tell you that if you try this out, it makes you feel immediately better and if it makes you feel better, why wouldn't you do it? This started me off on a more spiritual path, coinciding with me going all-in with the business and I started reading about the law of attraction, part of which is gratitude.

Gratitude is a funny one because in today's fast paced life, you actually need to stop what you are doing and look around to practise gratitude, and so many of us 'don't have time' for that. You need to make time for it. Let me tell you something about not having time... you do, you choose where you want to spend it. Everyone has time that they choose to use scrolling on Instagram, or watching Netflix and whilst there is nothing wrong with these things, I want you to be aware of where your time is actually going, especially when it comes to social media. So, if you have 10 minutes to mindless scroll on social media, you can definitely find 10 minutes to do your gratitude practise. Even get up 10 minutes earlier if you're in the 'don't have time' camp. Find somewhere nice to sit and think of 3 things you are grateful for right now, one after the other. These can range from being thankful for the roof over your head and the wonderful people in your life, to tiny things like the nice, cosy jammies you are wearing or how excellent this morning's cup of tea is. Spend a few minutes on each thing, really FEEL grateful for it. For me, this feels like the excited feeling I get in my stomach before I go on holiday and I believe this raises my mood and vibration and helps me attract greater experiences and opportunities into my life. I'm not going to go into the law of attraction because there are a million books on it, read "Deliberate Receiving" by Melody Fletcher or, of course, "The Secret" by Rhonda Byrne, but I believe this stuff works.

For me, the gratitude practice takes three forms: past, present, and future. I am grateful for things that have happened to me in the past - even the not so nice things - because they ultimately lead me to where I am today and pushed me onto this path. Let's use my situation after university as an example. When I left uni, I couldn't get a job anywhere. I was unemployed and on the dole twice because the job market was so rotten. I felt so bloody hard done by (spoiler alert: self-pity is bad vibes!). Every day, I was thinking "seriously, what did I actually do to deserve this?" I did everything I was supposed to, stuck in at school, went to uni and I was being rewarded with this baron shell of a job market with zero opportunities. Now, looking back, I can see that once I pulled myself out of the self-pity hole, there were still so many opportunities open to me, they just weren't the obvious ones like find a great job and stick at it. I often think if I had come out of uni and landed the dream job, I would never have started the business. I don't think I could have allowed myself to leave the safety of nice pay packet and I think now I would be in too deep with mortgages and real life to ever feel like I could leave and start a business. I also feel like this period of uncertainty was like entrepreneur training because my entire life is literally sprinkled with uncertainty and you need to learn to deal with it too. In fact, you need to learn to love it because at the other side of uncertainty is serious excitement and delight! So, I am often thankful, during my practise or as I reminisce about this time in my life, when in the moment, I actually felt like my whole world was falling down around me! Can you think of something in the past that has happened to you that actually, with hindsight you can see you had to go through to get to this point in business?

Then we have the present. Your new perspective on the past can be put to use here because you can use it to see the lessons in every situation or the direction you're being pushed in, which can make some scary business situations easier to deal with. For example, I have been negotiating a commercial lease on a property for the past 7 months. If you haven't negotiated a commercial lease before, it does take a long time but generally, 7 months is unreasonable. I wanted into the premises for October. It came and went. Then I settled for Christmas. Santa did not deliver. So I thought, ok, January... you can see where this is going. It's the end of Feb and we are still not in. This is frustrating as hell, let me tell you. We're also losing money every month because our current space is too small and our waiting lists for classes are as long as someone else's leg (I am 5ft, so not mine). So what's the positive here? Well, immediately I can't find one but I trust there is a reason and we, as a company, will be better off as a result of this delay. This might sound like mindless positivity but even if it turned out that nothing good came from this delay, the fact I thought something good would happen means I am less stressed and I am trusting the process rather than getting worked up about something I can do nothing about. What I am not suggesting here is you wander through business life without pushing to make things happen (I REALLY have been pushing and fighting to make this lease happen), but be grateful for the lessons and the direction you're being pushed in, not just in hindsight but in real time as it happens. If I was to hazard a guess about what the lesson is in this process for me, I would say that learning how to manage a lease negotiation that's going wrong is excellent experience for me as a franchisor as I will have to coach people to do the same. In my franchise business, I tend to say that I have made all the mistakes so they don't have to and I guess this is looking like another example of that!

The future is special and requires a bit of imagination and visualisation. How can you be grateful for things that haven't happened yet? That's madness, surely? It's not and it's a very useful and fun tool you can use to attract great things into your life. Let's say, for example, you have a dream client you would love to work with. You can visualise what that looks like in detail and be grateful in advance for it. It sounds weird, but saying thanks in advance seems to cement the idea in your mind as more possible than it was before and as a result, leave you more open to opportunities that will lead you towards making that situation a reality. I recently heard visualisation being described as making memories in the future and I just absolutely love that. My caveat here would be that it should be *just* out of the realms of what you think is possible now anyway. So, starting a business today and visualising that Elton John will phone you up and want to work with you is probably not going to work because you yourself would have to be an absolute fantasist to BELIEVE that could happen immediately, and for this to work, you need to believe that whilst currently out of reach, this thing is possible for you.

When you keep doing this and keep reaching and achieving what was originally just outside your grasp, the only thing that can happen is constant growth. You will push yourself and amaze yourself with what you are actually capable of, all through "living it" through your thoughts and as a result, being super open minded to opportunities. There is a great saying: "Where your attention goes, your energy flows". I don't know who said it, it was in a Disclosure song, but wherever it came from, it's true. Why don't you try this with something small. Is there someone just a little bit out of reach you can think of who has an aligned business to yours that you would like to collaborate with? Perhaps you are an indie skincare company and there is a micro influencer who you love who has an audience that you know would love your products. They're a little out of reach, so just messaging them and asking to collaborate wouldn't work. Start thinking about what this collaboration looks and feels like every day in your gratitude practice. Imagine seeing sales coming through on your website, using this persons unique discount code. Imagine forging a lasting relationship that benefits both of you for years to come. Be open to any opportunities that present themselves and watch that partnership come to life! I would LOVE to hear about these btw, please head to jennydrew.com and get in touch, let me know what your intentions were and how it all came together!

BEING OK WITH WANTING MORE

There is something weird about the way we are brought up in this society. I don't know if it's a British thing or a creative thing but we are all very guarded about our dreams and ambitions. We kind of keep them to ourselves or whisper the big dreams under our breath. Maybe you joke about them because you know you need to put them out there into the universe but you don't want to be judged for "getting too big for your boots".

I can remember one day, coming home from university, I was mid way through my 4th year dissertation and I must have been at the point before I wanted to leave the country to get out of completing it because I proclaimed that one day, I would like to be a published author. I studied Fashion Business. Most people for their dissertation decided to rework an existing study or an existing theory. We were actually advised to do this because then there would be a lot of information and data there already, all packaged up for us to read and give a different opinion. Looking back, I can see that they were encouraging us to do this because it's the easiest option if you want a pass. I don't actually think universities should be stifling creativity like this and it's a massive flaw as aren't universities supposed to be trailblazers who study new things and come up with new theories? You can probably guess that I did not decide to take this route. I was probably a total pain in the arse for my lecturers actually. I wasn't loud or annoying but I was constantly pushing the boundaries and going against advice, sometimes to my own detriment. A textbook entrepreneur though, right? I would love to tell you that my dissertation was one of those aforementioned trailblazing pieces of work that I believe universities should be encouraging but actually, it was so bad I nearly failed my entire degree as a result. I can barely remember what it was about exactly, that's how riveting it was - or maybe I've just blocked it out to protect myself because it was like death by a thousand cuts. The reason I'm telling you this is because despite this being the most painful body of work I had ever completed, and despite not enjoying the subject matter at all, it still inspired me to say out loud that I wanted to be a published author one day. As you might have noticed, that has ACTUALLY happened. Albeit with a very different subject matter and one I am fully confident and qualified to talk about and one that I actually love. Contrary to my dissertation, this book has flowed out of my brain like I was put on this earth to help people realise their business potential. Which is just as well because I don't think I could put myself through the pain of another punk fashion dissertation!

It must have been around 2009 when I uttered those words into the world. I can actually remember standing in my parents kitchen whilst saying it. I don't remember being taken very seriously at the time but you only have to believe in yourself to make something happen (and given my then track record with writing, I do not blame anyone for not taking notice!). The way in which this book has come into my life is unusual also. If it had been totally up to me to write the book off my own back and then go about finding someone to help me publish it, I know it wouldn't have happened - or at least not for a long time. But I joined a mastermind that had help with a book included, so all I had to do was write it and the publishing side would be taken care of. I didn't join the mastermind for this, I joined it for the connections, but isn't this a nice way for the universe to deliver something to me on a plate that I uttered 12 years ago! If a wee future fairy was to go back in time and tell my peers that I would be a published author, they would have laughed and laughed.

You will come up against resistance every step of the way. If you are straying from the path, your loved ones will want to protect you from the unknown but what they don't realise is that the unknown is as magical as it is scary. The ones who don't have your best interests at heart will want to keep you down at their level in case you do actually make it like you say you will, because those types of people cannot be happy for others until they do some serious self-development. Regardless of whether someone's intentions are good or bad, you need to stay true to yourself. Just before my business took off,

I was unemployed several times (thanks recession!). I was starting to look at graduate programs in supermarkets because I was under pressure to forge a career by those who loved me (and it did come from a place of love!). I can't even imagine how awful I would have been at that job. No one would have been winning, not me or the supermarket! Instead, I took a different path. I just KNEW there was something better out there for me. This was before there were books in my world about living your best life and programs on the TV about the law of attraction. I feel very fortunate that something in me had this blind faith that eventually it would all come good. I also have the grafting gene, which you will know comes in very useful in the first few years of business.

I want you to know that whatever you want in life is available to you. If someone else has it, why can't you have it too? If you can't believe it's possible, you're automatically closing doors of opportunity all over the place. Something that for me seems far-fetched is the super yacht I have on my horizon. It doesn't really get much more ridiculous than that, does it? I have a super yacht on my vision board, it's been on there for years. I won't take it off until I've either bought it (or some version of it) or decided I don't want it. The journey towards it has been fun in itself. In my accelerator program, from the early years of business, my mind was expanded by some people who taught me about the law of attraction and vision boards. I have had a vision board ever since. Early on I put a yacht on there. Originally it was probably for a bit of a laugh.

A few of us used to joke about the 'yacht club', who was going to get a boat first and what we could do to be intentional about this new boat life that was coming our way. Then I met a friend out with the accelerator who, you guessed it, had a boat. Not a super yacht by any means but a very nice boat at Loch Lomond in Scotland. He used to take me and my friends out on it and he taught us all to wakeboard too (still love this!). This vision board stuff was working. I then went to Ibiza and took photos of a super yacht with a helicopter on the roof. It is still my phone screensaver today - got to keep that dream alive and at the front of your mind!

A few years later, I decided I wanted to go somewhere exotic for my 30th birthday. My friend Nicki, who I met through networking, was up for coming with me. We ended up in Thailand on a super yacht because Nicki's friend's partner was the captain. We didn't stay on it, or go out in it, but normal folk can't just walk on to super yachts and have a wee wander about. Another few years later, I'm in Marbella with family and friends. It was our friend's birthday, we managed to rent a yacht and crew for the day and because there were so many of us it was just within budget. It was probably one of the best days I have ever had on the water.

Do you think I'm having some pretty extraordinary boat experiences by luck or because I'm open to opportunities and in some cases, actively pulling it into my life? If you think it's luck then you will continue to wander through life unintentionally letting things happen to you rather than positively influencing your life's direction. If even 1% of you thinks this could be intentional then what do you have to lose by trying this intentional attraction yourself?

There is so much abundance in the world and it's yours for the taking if you can master your own mindset. When I say abundance I mean of everything: happiness, friendships, nature, experiences and money.

Talking about money might make you feel uncomfortable. It's a very British thing, that. We don't talk about our wages, we don't talk about how much things cost. This all changed for me when I started the business and started pitching my business idea, including financial figures, to rooms full of people. Suddenly, in this space, there was no taboo around money. In fact, you were encouraged to share your turnover, your net profit, your dividends, your tax bill. Suddenly, no financial question was off limits and I can tell you, it was so freeing. With my business friends and with some of my non business friends (although it might make them squirm) I will ask about and talk about money. It's just a token to be exchanged for things or services. When you break money down into what it really is, it takes the sting out of it. If you're not earning as much as the next person, it's not because you're not as good as them; you're either at an earlier stage of business, or you're still tweaking your model to make it work, or you're still really trying to find your thing. No one person should ever be valued by how much money they make or have in the bank. If you have found success and managed to build a nice life for yourself, it should be your duty to educate and help others on their journey, if they so wish, to follow in your footsteps. If you're in a position where you can create fulfilling employment for people then I believe you should do that too, especially if you yourself have experienced questionable jobs in the past.

By striving to make more money, you're not being greedy (as society might make you feel) as long as you're open to doing good things and helping people along the way. You're not a horrible Cruella DeVille type character for lusting after a healthier bank balance. Money buys you choice and freedom. It buys you nice things as well but you soon realise it's the experiences and helping other people that are the real reward. Make sure that whatever your business is sits comfortably with you morally. Are you solving your customers' problems? Are you creating experiences that make them feel good? Are they better off with your business in their life than without? I always find asking yourself these questions not only keeps your business on the straight and narrow but also allows you to justify taking the nice wage, buying the nice car, going on the nice holiday. If you're ripping people off, selling poor quality products and delivering sub-par services then I think you will find that not only is your business unsustainable, but also, ultimately you will not be happy or fulfilled. Fix this before your reputation is damaged; you can do better!

Once you start growing, you will inevitably come up against people who aren't very happy about it - it's an occupational hazard of having a successful business. I touched on this a bit earlier but they usually sit in two camps: the ones who love you and are scared of the unknown on your behalf and the ones who fear you will leave them behind. The ones who love you just need to be convinced of your vision. Tell them your plan, give them this book to read, help them understand that if there's more to life for you then there is also more to life for them. I'm not saying you should be telling your Auntie Jo to quit her job and start a business, but I can bet Auntie Jo would benefit from a wee vision board next to her dressing table. Vision boards aren't exclusively reserved for business owners you know - they work for everyone! If you are up against resistance with your loved ones then you might be a trailblazer in your family. You've maybe already been a trailblazer by being the first person to go to uni or the first person to visit other continents. This journey you're on will benefit and inspire everyone. When you start to reap the rewards of a successful business, you'll be taking them along for the ride and helping and inspiring future generations too. So whilst you are convincing them to get on board with your vision, know that it's ok if they don't actually get it until there's something tangible, like a big order, for them to actually see.

As for the ones who want to hold you back out of fear you will leave them behind - know it's not about you. They have some work to be done on their own mindset and insecurities. Some of these people you will outgrow and leave behind and that's ok. Some of them you will inspire and they will come round to your way of thinking. Again - give them this book. It might make them understand more about what you are trying to achieve. Not everyone will get on board with what you're trying to achieve and that's ok. Be mindful of not spending too much time in the negative energy spaces - don't cut out everyone who doesn't blindly get on board but don't choose to stay in that space too much either.

And I suppose there is a third type of person, the ones who are easy-osy and aren't really that interested in what you're doing business wise - these folk are often a refreshing tonic. You can hang about with them and just be a human being who wants to have a cup of tea and a laugh and not talk about any heavy duty life plans. You need these people too.

One caveat I have here, before you put people into categories, is you do need to be aware that you're not always going to be right. There are some serious things that you should heed if your family are stepping in. You should not get yourself into horrendous debt and get mad at your family for not getting on board with your vision. You should not do anything to the detriment of your physical or mental health and get mad at your family for not getting on board with the vision. In this, I include constant high stress - it is NOT good for you. Family/friends and your health is important, so make sure you don't lose sight of that. Your business won't be successful if you're not healthy and happy enough to run it!

Finally, I want to touch on something I think is very important and that is staying grounded despite your success. You will be successful, if you can see it and you can believe it then it's yours for the taking. Make sure you stay humble along the way. Make time for people who need your help, do good things, help people build their version of your success. Don't take yourself too seriously and enjoy the journey!! I just spent a week in LA with some very accomplished business owners (more so than I am). You might think that sounds a bit dry but my aim in social situations has always been, and will always be, to have a laugh and that's exactly what we did, for a whole week. Money isn't everything, success isn't everything, but being happy and healthy is so don't lose sight of that.

PRICING FOR YOUR CUSTOMER EXPERIENCE

Pricing is one of the trickiest parts of business, especially if you are a creative and I would also add especially if you are a woman. We are very humble about our value, and don't want to be seen to be "too big for our boots" by charging more than the next person. Before we delve into the world of pricing though, we need to really understand why people buy from you.

There are two main reasons people buy: to increase pleasure or to decrease pain. You might sit firmly in one of these camps or you might find your product or service falls into both categories. Examples of increasing pleasure would be making new friends, learning a new skill that boosts your confidence, feeling good in a new item of clothing, showing that you can afford to spend a certain amount of money (vanity) etc. Examples of decreasing pain would be doing something to help you de-stress, going to a class that helps you get fit to increase your health, hiring someone to help clean your house so you have more time, finding ways to save your money so you feel more financially secure etc. In order to price correctly and to sell your product or service, you need to understand who your customer is, and what their drivers for purchasing your product or service are in the first place.

When I started my business, pricing was a total guess because not that many people were actually running sewing classes so I didn't have many competitors UK wide to look to. I actually think this was a good thing because one of the worst things you can do is price yourself in line with a competitor and assume they are a business guru who has done all the research that you are about to do now. When I started Sew Confident, I worked for a few small businesses on the side. The decision to work for small companies was firstly, because they tend to be more flexible with my hours and secondly, because I knew I could learn a lot from them working on the inside. I didn't work for any competitors (like I said, they didn't really exist), I worked for a men's high end retailer at the time, called Fat Buddha Store. The owner, Leslie, was quite interested in what I was doing, which now I get because if I ever have staff members with a side hustle, I'm always interested to know what they are up to and see if I can offer any nuggets of wisdom! At the very start, I remember telling Leslie what I was going to offer and what I was going to charge. My beginners class was going to run from 10-4 over two consecutive Saturdays or Sundays, and I was going to charge £90 per head. It included lunch, which was £4.50 per head. The room fee was £15 per hour so for a full class over 2 days, I was looking to make £504 which was £42 per hour. To me at the time, this was CRAZY MONEY. But there were a lot of things I wasn't factoring in. First, I wasn't considering the time spent preparing for the class, or creating the class, or marketing the class, or emailing customers about the class. I wasn't factoring in petrol or parking and the drive time going there and back. I wasn't factoring in the time it would take me to carry 8 machines and boxes of tools up and down to my car from my second story flat and I also wasn't building in any margin for the future to be able to pay someone else to take the class whilst I grow the business or teach elsewhere. In addition, I wasn't factoring in tax or insurance, or any of the other standard business overheads. Straight off the bat, Leslie said - that's too cheap. He suggested at least £150. I mean there was no way I could charge that, even though I knew I was good at this, probably the best at it, even then. And I knew I had developed and tested all my classes in my previous job and tweaked and improved them in line with customer feedback. Even though I knew I was going to be able to ensure that every single person who stepped into my class would leave happier and lighter, having forgotten anything they were worried about, with new friends and life-long skills, I still couldn't charge that. Then he said something to me I will always remember - "It's easier to reduce your prices than put them up". To this day, I find myself reiterating this. It sticks in my mind whenever I am chatting to a new business about price because it's so true. I was so worried about pricing myself out of the market (what market?!?! It didn't exist!!) that I finally managed to push my prices up to £115. And it felt uncomfortable... until people started paying it without batting an eyelid. What was I so afraid of? I was in the classic lack mindset of the new entrepreneur. Why would they pay me for this? Why will they pay me more than the local college that's running classes for £80 for a 12 week term? Who do I think I am charging this kind of money? How can I sleep at night knowing I've taken people's hard earned cash and now I'm spending it on myself. Whatever thoughts you have had in the past about pricing, I can guarantee I've had them too. Our brains have a bias towards the negative, it's why the feeling of "what if tomorrow everyone stops buying from me?" never truly goes away, so get used to coaching yourself out of that mindset... sometimes it's necessary on a daily basis!

To really feel good about pricing, you need to really believe that your product or service is solving a real problem for your customers. That might look like making them feel good when they go on a night out with a new dress. The problem was they wanted to feel great and had no dresses that would make them feel that way until they found your product. Or maybe it's helping their child pass their exams with ease, relieving stress for the kid and the parents and helping the child excel at school. The problem being the kid was falling behind, everyone was getting stressed out it was affecting the parent and child relationships and affecting their child's mental health at school. Two very different problems. One seems frivolous and one seems serious. I used these examples because when I use the word "problem", I don't want your brain going straight to "create world peace". You can still impact your customers' lives with a clothing brand as much as you can help a child get through school with their mental health intact. If you are reading this just now and you've fallen into a trap of selling sub-par products to try and make a fast buck so you can pay your rent, I am not judging you but I am urging you to change direction. To build a sustainable business that will fulfil you, you need to be passionate about the problem you are solving. If your only reason for being in business is to fleece people for money you'll either be broke and miserable or rich and miserable. Either way, you'll be miserable (money DEFINITELY does not fix miserable!). If you're not sure what your problem is, connect with me on social media - all my info can be found here;

www.jennydrew.com I can help!

Once you have figured out the problem you are solving, you should have a better idea of who your customer is. Your customer is never "everyone" btw. Let's say you are selling beautiful embroidered bedspreads. You could argue that technically everyone who owns a bed is your customer because they will need a version of your product, but 55-year-old John, who lives on his own, is definitely not interested in spending much money on his bed sheets and you can guarantee he doesn't really care what they look like. You need to zero in on your customer so you can get to know them and make your products or services known to them. The Sew Confident customer, for example, is 25-45 professional female. If I was asked to zero in even more, I would reduce that age range to 35-45. Do we have customers out with this age range? Absolutely! Do we have customer who are retired, or stay-at-home mums, men or people otherwise wouldn't put themselves in the "professional female" bracket? Of course! They are not any less welcome in our classes but our marketing efforts are not specifically aimed at them as we have discovered our main market is this 25-45 professional female.

Once you know the problem you are solving and who your customer is, you can start to think a bit more about what your prices should look like. Remember, money is just a token that is exchanged for goods or services that the buyer deems to be appropriate. Too expensive or too cheap and you'll hit problems. There is a relationship between price and perceived value. I can actually remember learning about this in uni and now I see it playing out in real life every day. Let's say you are looking to go to an art class. You've researched a bit and found one class that's £5 per 2 hour class and another that's £24 per 2 hour class. They SEEM to promise the same kind of thing, but there must be a reason the price is different. Maybe the £5 class has loads of people and you won't get much help, or maybe the tutor isn't very good and that's why they're not charging very much. You can afford the £24, so you pay it. Can you remember a time where, as a consumer, you have gone for the higher price option because you assumed there might be something sub-par about the cheaper option? I bet you can! You need to bear this in mind when you are setting your prices. There is a direct correlation between your prices and the perceived quality of your services or products. The keyword here is "perceived" because they don't have much to go from other than price and maybe some reviews if they do some digging. Both classes could well be the same quality, but the higher price class might be making more sales because of price alone - is that the opposite of what you thought would be the case? It certainly used to be for me.

The next part of this puzzle is actual value. Your prices will create the impression of value but if you don't live up to those expectations, you're going to be in trouble. So, where can you add value to justify your prices and make people feel that they made the right choice going for the more expensive version? This is where you can really excel if you put your mind to it. Let's take the art classes example. You are the £24 per 2 hour class version. You justify this price to yourself and your customers because you only use beautiful venues with nice coffee and wine. You know your customer is (probably the same as mine) 35-45 professional female, so you are never using community centres with their dreary lighting and setting because that doesn't align with your customer who would never normally frequent a community centre. You've recognised that one of the reasons your customers are looking for art classes is to meet new people, so you ensure that you facilitate conversation within the group and you provide an online community for them to stay in touch with you and their peers (this is also good for keeping them engaged with you and your brand for future selling). You also know they are time poor so you make sure there are kits for them to buy to take home so they can continue their hobby straight away without having to trawl the internet hoping they are buying the right tools and materials.

In this example, there are lots of things that justify the higher price to me if I was the customer. The venue is a nicer place to visit, I can get a nice wine whilst I paint. The company talks about the social side of painting so I know it's going to be easier to meet new people there and it won't be an unfriendly environment. The company has kits I can buy so if I want to continue painting at home, I can get started straight away and know that I have all the right tools and materials. There could be other things at play here too. Perhaps I want to be seen to be going to the most expensive art class so people know I can afford it (vanity is a massive driver for a lot of people when purchasing!). Perhaps I have been told by a doctor that I need to do something mindful to decrease my stress levels or my health will suffer, so I need the best art class I can find because health is everything.

There will be lots of factors that make your customer pay a certain amount. You need to map out the value of the product or the service you are providing. If you already have customers, I would suggest a survey or a focus group. They have all the answers you are looking for so why not ask them rather than guessing? You might be surprised to find out their reasons for being a customer. I think it was about 2 or 3 years into my business when I was advised to survey the customers - not just for class feedback but to ask them why they wanted to come to classes in the first place, how it made them feel and what else we could do or provide to make their experience better. You can ask people about their profession, their household income, the biggest worry they have in their life etc. Always do this anonymously, give them the option not to answer any of the questions they feel uncomfortable with and reward them for taking part in your survey with a discount code or entry into a prize draw (they will need to email you upon completion to keep the survey anonymous). If you've never surveyed your customers before and you've been in business for more than 3 months, you need to survey them today! I have a template for you on the website;

www.jennydrew.com/bookbonus

because I know it can be a laborious task to create all the questions. When I first did this, I discovered that people were coming to my classes to de-stress. I now talk about this all the time and we have a massive emphasis on reminding people to find time for themselves and a mindful activity like sewing a couple of times a week.

Once you have validated the problem you are solving with your survey and you've perhaps found out some other problems you can solve, you can justify your pricing. When you discover that your art class isn't just about learning how to paint, it's the whole experience, it's improving your customers wellbeing, it's growing their social circle, it's increasing their confidence, then you can justify being the most expensive art class in the city. You can shout about why you are the best place for art classes. To do this, you do need to be genuinely passionate about the change you are creating for people. If you genuinely believe that the service you are providing is solving your customers problems, improving their wellbeing etc., you will be able to sell the classes knowing your value is way more than just an art teacher and you deserve to be paid according to the time, effort and care you are putting into your service. You will also feel super satisfied in your work if you are earning a wage that enables you to have a nice life and do the things you want to do. If you charge too little, you will eventually resent your customers for not paying enough and you will feel undervalued… even though YOU set the prices! Believe me, this will happen. So pricing correctly will also increase the sustainability of your business from a you-won't-get-fed-up-and-want-to-pack-it-all-in sense as well as financially!

What if people start messaging you saying they love the sound of your classes but they can't afford them. It doesn't actually matter how much you charge, you will always get these messages. On rare occasions, if combined with a drop in sales, you might have priced yourself too high or be marketing yourself at the wrong audience. Your price point has to match your target audience; if there's a disconnect between what that audience can afford (or want to pay) and what you are charging then sales will drop. You either need to tweak your pricing or tweak your marketing and audience. Most of the time though, the "I can't afford you" message is from someone who isn't your customer. Not everyone will be able to afford you and that's ok. It's not your duty to be affordable to everyone, in fact, it's impossible. If they can't afford you, they can afford the £5 art class down the road or the college courses that are always cheaper because they are subsidised charities. I know in Scotland there are a lot of courses you can do for free at colleges - you can point them towards these options. When I speak to a business owner who I can see is pained by these messages, I use the Ferrari example. I would love a Ferrari btw. I cannot afford one. If I went into a Ferrari dealership and said "I would really like this SF90 Spider please but I can't afford it", do you think they would spend all day feeling bad that they didn't have a product I could afford? No, because I am not their customer. I have never even seen a Ferrari advert anywhere other than whilst watching the F1. They don't advertise on the TV because that's not where their customers hang out... they DO hang out at the F1 though - in the good seats! My point is, knowing when someone isn't your customer is just as valuable as recognising who IS your customer. If you spend your time trying to serve absolutely everyone, you will dilute your business and your messaging until it resonates with no one at all, and you'll drive yourself mad in the process.

The biggest takeaway from this chapter should be that you are definitely providing more of a service than you think. You need to get inside the mind of your customer and find out what they need and how you can provide added value to them. This will allow you to charge your worth and will create a community of customers who come back time and time again because they know you genuinely care about them. I hope this chapter makes you do the work and increase your pricing in line with your value today!

GROWTH ROAD HUMPS

There comes a point in every ambitious entrepreneur's journey where you hit a bump in the road that forces you to up your game. I call these 'Growth Road Humps' and let me tell you, I am very familiar with them... in fact, I'm standing right before one in my own business journey right now. My definition of a Growth Road Hump is an event in your business journey that almost feels insurmountable but you fight through it and come out the other side a better version of yourself, or with a stronger business model.

Growth Road Humps(GRH) are uncomfortable, often stressful, and almost always scary until you get over the other side and you can see how much you learned, have grown and have progressed as a result of it. The first real GRH I remember experiencing was when I had made the decision to take on a premises. I had been using 3rd party venues to run my sewing classes and one month, I paid out so much money to these venues it became ludicrous to keep using them as I could take on a full time premises for less. There were lots of benefits to starting my business in this way. It was almost risk free. I had mobility within the city in regard to where I could run classes, I could test out different styles of venue, different catering options(I used to include lunches in my classes back then!). I also had nothing to pay if I went on holiday and nothing was tying me to Glasgow if I decided to leave. But I also had no real skin in the game, and that can make you complacent and stifle growth. All in was the only option. I started looking for my own venue of some sort - I didn't exactly know what I was looking for but at the back of my mind, I was feeling pretty terrified of what would happen if it all went tits up and I had signed this legally binding contract saying I would pay the rent for 5 years. My catastrophising brain at the time had me out on the street with nothing, paying the rent with my kidneys - thankfully I have worked on that brain and it no longer shows me that image - it used to be a yearly occurrence! The first thing I did to limit my liability was to become a limited company. That meant this business entity was the one taking the risk, not me. The second thing that put my mind at slight ease was I found a landlord who was keen to encourage arty people to make a go of it and as a result, had made the lease super easy to understand and not that scary. It wasn't a full repairing and insuring lease for a start (I would have run for the hills if that had been my only option!). Despite all this mitigation of risk, I was still terrified to take this leap but I was also super excited for what it meant for me and the company. I had tested this model for two years. It worked and a premise was the next obvious step. You know what happens next, I, of course, took the lease and the company went from strength to strength. We weren't limited by what I could fit in my car, equipment wise, I was no longer having to humph machines everywhere and we were able to create this lovely creative happy place for our customers that was also significantly less expensive for the business per hour, thus making us way more profitable!

Looking back at this, it seems such a small thing and some of you might be reading this thinking it's small potatoes as well, but for me back then, it was huge and scary. But it was also all part of my growth, personally. It was exercising the calculated risk muscle which, I can tell you, still needs work today but is in much better shape, having made a lot of scary decisions over the years - not all of which have paid off btw! But I do remember finally feeling like I had a 'real business', like I was more worthy of success now because I had been brave and done something that a lot of people will never do and have never done. Something in me changed for sure and something in you will change every time you overcome one of these GRHs. I don't think I was right to suddenly feel like I was a "real business" owner because I had a bricks and mortar premise - that's a lot of nonsense - but rightly or wrongly, it created a shift in my mindset which as a result, made me dream bigger and push the business forward... until the next GRH of course!

Don't worry, I'm not going to write several paragraphs on every single one - that's a whole book in itself but the ones that stick out for me are:

- Taking on my first employee
- Building the franchise model
- Teaching on live TV every month for over a year
- Investing £15k in a business mastermind
- Launching our online classes in a pandemic
- Travelling to Ibiza to meet business people I didn't know (also in a pandemic).

And the one I am currently standing in front of is, of course, opening a high street shop version of Sew Confident, which could change the entire landscape of our franchise offering and entire business going forward. You'll need to keep an eye on my socials to see how that one turns out!

I bet as you read this, you yourself can identify your own personal GRHs. You can probably remember how you felt before hand and how you felt afterwards. You might even be able to recognise some that didn't exactly go your way but I bet you still changed and grew as a person and a business owner.

It's really useful to look back at your past achievements and challenges in order to help you overcome the future challenges. I don't want you to dwell on the past but even in the most disastrous of experiences, there will be lessons you had to learn that make you a better business owner now. I know that doing this often trains your brain to reframe challenges in your head almost as they're happening so you can skip the weeks of despair! It's also incredibly important to look back on your past achievements. This is something we do not do enough. We can be too busy moving on to the next thing to celebrate the current thing and I truly believe that kind of disregard for your own achievements in the moment will eventually make you wonder why the hell you're even doing this in the first place.

How do you motivate yourself to push past the tough bits of the GRH? This is a very individual thing and you will know yourself what motivates you and what a suitable reward at the other side could be. The reward has to be relative to the road hump as well. For example, back in the pre-premises days I wouldn't have said to myself "once I get this premises open, I'm going to buy myself a Porsche", because the value of the Porsche would have been considerably more than the profit I would have made on the premises opening. So make sure the reward is relative to the return you get after the GRH.

I have rewarded myself with all kinds of things over the years. Some things were expensive like my Louis Vuitton handbag (still only about 2.5% of the profit I made after the GRH) and some things were very cheap like one Quality Street chocolate after every 20 minutes of solid work accomplished. I've also rewarded myself in the past with nice overnight stays, or even allowing myself extra days off work to sit in the sun after I've worked hard to overcome something!

Something I really do want to mention here is a mistake I have made in the past. I told myself I was going to buy that handbag once I sold my first franchise, then my second, then my third. All of these things came and went and still I hadn't bought the handbag. It got to the point where my husband was intervening like "CAN YOU PLEASE JUST BUY THE

HANDBAG ALREADY AND STOP TALKING ABOUT IT". It was like I had made a deal with myself but continued to move the goalposts. If I was employed by myself I would be ragin' with this. Constantly changing my mind. Make sure you treat yourself like your most prized employee - especially in the early days. Don't break promises to yourself, reward yourself for the hard work and praise yourself! Eventually, I bought the handbag after the online Capsule Collection course success. Perhaps the issue I had here was the relative price of the bag vs the profit from the GRH didn't sit well with me, but I know I was doing myself a disservice by not acknowledging that I was achieving big things.

It's easy as an entrepreneur to just move onto the next thing. Maybe it's something to do with our success or our humble nature… I know not all entrepreneurs are like this but most of the female creative ones I have met certainly are. I want you to know that it's ok to think you're doing well. Just like it's ok to think you deserve better, and to go after that massive success unapologetically.

Find something that will push you towards the big goals but also find something that will push you towards the wee ones - those are easier to overcome and their bite size nature makes them a regular win which our reward centric brains really thrive on these days.

Let's talk about the elephant in the Growth Road Hump room here. How do you know when a situation is something you should push to get through or a sign you should be diverting in another direction or stopping what you are doing altogether? This is a tough one and there is a lot to be said for really trusting your gut here.

I don't want you to read this chapter and assume that every time it gets hard you should always push through, throwing resources, and time at every obstacle regardless of the outcome. Just as I don't want you to read this chapter and assume that whenever it gets hard you should quit. Instead, I want you to know that whenever it gets hard, you need to reevaluate the situation, listen to your gut, look at the pros and cons of the obstacle and take action once you have gathered all the knowledge you can. Ask yourself why you're doing it. Is it because you believe, given the evidence, that it's going to grow your business or you as an entrepreneur? If so, do it. Has an unbelievable opportunity presented itself to you that wasn't part of the plan but will grow you as a business or entrepreneur? If so, do it! Can you get over this GRH without diverting too many resources or too much cash away from your bread and butter business income? If so, do it!

Or are you doing it because you think it's expected of you and you don't want to disappoint anyone? That's a red flag that needs to be delved into a bit deeper (everyone needs a therapist - get one!). Are you looking at competitors, seeing what they are doing and following their models blindly, even when it doesn't exactly feel right to you? And finally, if you are a new business, in the first few years you should always be open to the possibility that your business as it is now might not be the finally version, there may be some pivoting to come, or you might end up decided something else entirely is where you should be spending your time and that is ok. You need to have a very honest, measured, non-emotional conversation with yourself before deciding what you're going to do about the GRHs. How you do this will depend on the kind of person you are. If you're an impulsive person, you need to sit with this idea until it's really digested. If you're very risk averse, you need to recognise in yourself when you're running away from something out of fear of the unknown even when you can see that the outcome if you push through would be amazing for you and the business.

I've mentioned before that it took me several business ideas before I found the one that worked. Had I clung on for dear life to the first business (bespoke homewares) or the second idea (bespoke tights!) - I wouldn't be writing this book now. However, if I had kept jumping from idea to idea to idea, I also wouldn't be writing this book now. I am someone with magpie tendencies, I can be impulsive, I can struggle to see things through and I can be risk averse. Yet I've negotiated many GRHs successfully. I can acknowledge that these are some traits that I can be affected by but at the end of the day, I am aware of them and I have the power to overcome and override them when I need to. Being aware of your default traits in business and not letting them define you as a person so you can override them when you need to is a really powerful tool. So don't use these traits as an excuse to bow out when it gets tough. Never say "ah well, you know, that's what I'm like" as if you have no control over your tendencies to procrastinate, or to work yourself into burnout. Take responsibility, you're in control, and every seemingly negative behaviour you recognise always has a positive. My magpie tendencies keep me open to inspiration from my surroundings all the time. So I can come up with ideas that grow from things I am picking up in my environment that no one else can pick up on. My impulsive tendencies, when well managed, can make me take action. I can fix things quickly and step in before things spiral out of control. And leaning towards being more risk averse than a risk taker means I calculate the risks involved in everything I do. It means I've had steady, sustained growth in the business, year on year. So every behaviour that you might see as blocking your progress has a positive too. You just need to be aware of what yours are.

I've had Growth Road Humps that have made me give up businesses altogether - like not making enough money and having to decide whether to get finance to grow or pack it in. I've had growth road humps that I've pushed through even though every step of the way (in hindsight) even when my gut was telling me not to do it - like the second studio I opened that I closed a year later. And I've had growth road humps that have moved the business forward, really put us on the map and allowed other people to get a slice of this amazing creative business owner life - like creating the UK's only sewing tuition franchise. There have been positives and negatives from all of these experiences. I have learned so much of what to do and what not to do - a lot of which is now in this book! I can't tell you how many times I ask myself "why are you doing this to yourself" as I once again take on what seems like more than I can chew. But when things get easy, I get bored and seek the thrill of building and creating new things.

And I'm on the journey with you, It doesn't matter how big the business gets, you're always negotiating big, scary, growth road humps. It's all part of this super exciting, sometimes terrifying, rewarding and privileged journey of entrepreneurship!

Buckle up, shit's gonna get wild!

AFTERWORD

I feel like I should be singing a wee farewell song by this point in the book, but I know this is actually just the start for you, the start for us as we embark on this crazy journey together!

My main aim for this book is to inspire women in creative businesses to realise that what they THINK they are capable of is just the tip of the iceberg. I wanted to illuminate the inevitable ceilings you will hit and enable you to believe in your ability to absolutely smash them to smithereens. Throughout my journey I have struggled against stereotypes, against gender bias, against my own mindset and against society's idea of what I should be doing, what I should be earning and the tables I should be sitting at. The biggest thing I have learned is that it's MY decision to choose what I want to do, it's my decision how much I should earn and it's my decision what table I should be sitting at or actually who gets to sit at mine.

You get to sit at my table. I will tell you all day long that you're worthy and capable of wild success, that you're better than you even know, that great, exciting times are ahead of you and that now is your time to Stop Playing Small.

ACKNOWLEDGMENTS

To my husband Steve - thank you for always believing I can do whatever I put my mind to and never being shocked when I pull it off. For the copious amount of tea you made for me whilst writing this and for the extra dog walks you went on even when it was my turn. I couldn't ask for a better partner in crime than you, love you always!

And to my FFF girls, Christine, Margaret and Louise - thank you for your consistent support through the good and the bad times. Always being on hand with some sterling advice, a giggle and a bottle of prosecco - inspiring me every day to aim higher. Your friendship is so precious to me. See you on the yacht!

ABOUT THE AUTHOR

Jenny Drew

Jenny Drew is a multi award winning business owner and creator of the UK's only sewing tuition franchise.

Jenny believes that when given the right tools, women in the creative space can create extraordinary businesses that enhance the lives of those around them and so she helps these women navigate the business landscape to create serious success.

Work With Jenny

If you'd like to work with Jenny or get in touch please visit www.jennydrew.com

Printed in Great Britain
by Amazon

17742812R00079